Visualizing Health
and Healthcare Data

Visualizing Health and Healthcare Data

Creating Clear and Compelling Visualizations to "See How You're Doing"

Katherine Rowell
Lindsay Betzendahl
Cambria Brown

WILEY

Published by John Wiley & Sons, Inc., Hoboken, New Jersey.

Published simultaneously in Canada.

For general information on our other products and services or for technical support, please contact our Customer Care Department within the United States at (800) 762-2974, outside the United States at (317) 572-3993, or fax (317) 572-4002.

Wiley publishes in a variety of print and electronic formats and by print-on-demand. Some material included with standard print versions of this book may not be included in e-books or in print-on-demand. If this book refers to media such as a CD or DVD that is not included in the version you purchased, you may download this material at http://booksupport.wiley.com. For more information about Wiley products, visit www.wiley.com.

Library of Congress Cataloging-in-Publication Data:
Names: Rowell, Katherine L., author. | Betzendahl, Lindsay, author. | Brown, Cambria, author.
Title: Visualizing health and healthcare data : creating clear and compelling visualizations to "see how you're doing" / by Katherine Rowell, Lindsay Betzendahl, Cambria Brown.
Description: First edition. | Hoboken, New Jersey : Wiley, [2020] | Includes bibliographical references and index.
Identifiers: LCCN 2020032174 (print) | LCCN 2020032175 (ebook) | ISBN 9781119680888 (paperback) | ISBN 9781119682325 (adobe pdf) | ISBN 9781119680864 (epub)
Subjects: LCSH: Medical statistics—Data processing. | Information visualization.
Classification: LCC RA409.5 .R69 2020 (print) | LCC RA409.5 (ebook) | DDC 610.2/1—dc23
LC record available at https://lccn.loc.gov/2020032174
LC ebook record available at https://lccn.loc.gov/2020032175

Cover Design and artwork: Wiley

Printed in the United States of America.

SKY10021367_092520

Contents

Preface

We understand the challenges you face when trying to communicate health and healthcare data. We wrote this book to share our deep experience and expertise in creating clear, compelling, and actionable displays of health and healthcare data that empower people to "see how they're doing."

As a group, we've spent the last 30 years working on this book—29 conducting the research, and one writing it. Our research can be categorized into three areas: formal education, work experience, and self-education.

We've each had the privilege of a formal education delivered by recognized health and healthcare experts and thought leaders. This education is foundational to our ability to think critically about the various aspects of what health is, how health and healthcare systems operate, and the structures and policies that influence it all.

We've played a role in the development, capture, and analysis of just about every type of health and healthcare data imaginable—from administrative claims data to risk-adjusted clinical outcomes data to complex public health survey data. We've deciphered the inner workings of innumerable transactional systems and untangled databases created by evil geniuses.

Each of us can describe the moment we were bitten by the data visualization bug and set on a path of self-education. We sought out thought leaders in the field—some we know only through their books and blogs; others we have developed lifelong professional and personal friendships with. We learned and honed our viz skills through deep practice—stretching ourselves outside our comfort zone, stopping to reflect on successes and errors, making adjustments, and continuing the process over time. As a result, we have proudly joined the ranks of recognized data visualization experts, and we work with leading health and healthcare organizations throughout the world. And now, we have written this book to share our experience and expertise with you.

This book is organized into three sections. Section I is focused on understanding different types of data to be displayed, and requirement-gathering methods. All too often teams want to jump directly to creating displays, but this is a mistake to be avoided. Before you can determine how to display data and information, you must understand what will be displayed and for whom.

Section II provides an overview of the research that informs the best practices of table and graph design. Included in this chapter are the four fundamental shapes you can use alone or in combination to create clear and compelling displays of data. This section also includes detailed examples of the most common mistakes people make in selecting a chart type, with explanations about why they don't work, and examples of what works better and why.

Section III of the book defines and describes the characteristics of dashboards, reports, multidimensional exploratory displays (MEDS™) and infographics. It includes examples of each type of display and tips and tricks to designing and building them.

We ardently believe that making the message and the story in the data clear will improve health and healthcare systems. We hope this book will help you to join in our efforts.

Establishing a Framework and Process

"If you can't describe what you're doing as a process, you don't know what you're doing."

—W. Edwards Deming,
American engineer,
statistician, and leading quality
management thinker

Chapter One

Health and Healthcare Data Visualizations of Historical Importance

Even before modern-day visualization research validated the direct and powerful relationship between the way information is presented and the way we see and understand it, pioneering healthcare statisticians and caregivers like John Snow (1813–1858) and Florence Nightingale (1820–1910) understood that visual display could be a highly effective method for grasping and communicating the messages buried in data. No one who has ever taken an epidemiology course can forget Dr. John Snow's classic work, *On the Mode of Communication of Cholera*. By mapping the London street addresses of residents who had become sick (and in many cases died) and their distance from City water pumps, Snow could visually and effectively communicate the relationship between a single pathogen-tainted water source and the homes of people who contracted the disease. Most people who had fallen ill, it turned out, lived near the Broad Street pump. Snow persuaded the town council to remove the pump's handle, and the outbreak abated.

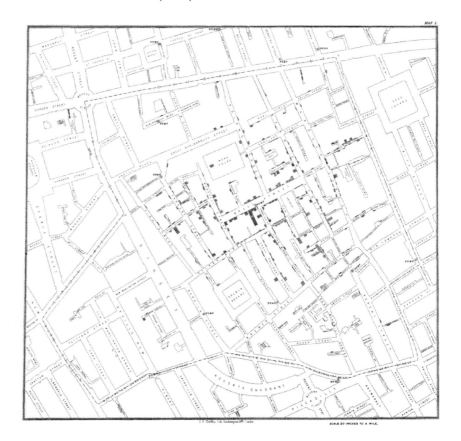

In 1868, British nurse Florence Nightingale—distressed by the alarmingly high mortality rates in the Crimean War—began to compile statistics on causes of death. Her analysis revealed that of the 900,000 soldiers who died during the war—more than half of 1,650,000 combatants from all countries involved—most had succumbed to preventable diseases arising from unsanitary conditions in the hospitals where they were treated, and not as a direct result of battlefield wounds. Nightingale recognized the buried message: better hygiene could have saved—and could still save—thousands of lives.

As impressive as her statistics were, Nightingale worried that the tables she presented to Queen Victoria would seem tedious, even incomprehensible, and feared that members of the British Parliament were unlikely to be swayed by numbers lying flat on a page. So Nightingale devised ingenious ways of presenting the information in charts.

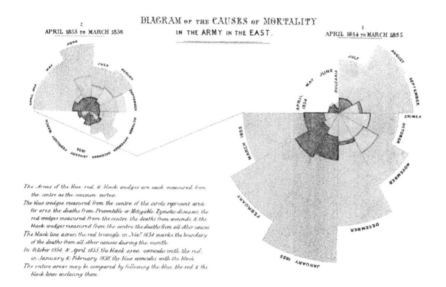

In the now-famous "Diagram of the Causes of Mortality in the Army in the East," each month is represented as a twelfth of a circle. The months with more deaths are shown with longer wedges so that the area of each wedge represents the total number of deaths. Preventable deaths are blue, deaths due to wounds are red, and deaths from all other causes are black. Over the months after March 1855, when members of the Sanitary Commission began repairing, cleaning, and otherwise improving field hospital conditions, the blue wedges shrank dramatically. Showing incredible insight into the power of displaying the data in this way, Nightingale said her graph was designed "to affect thro' the Eyes what we fail to convey to the public through their word-proof ears."

More recent efforts by healthcare researchers like those led by Dr. Jack Wennberg at the Dartmouth Atlas Project have documented glaring—and, for the most part, inexplicable—variations in how medical resources are apportioned and delivered in the United States. The project builds on Medicare data to provide

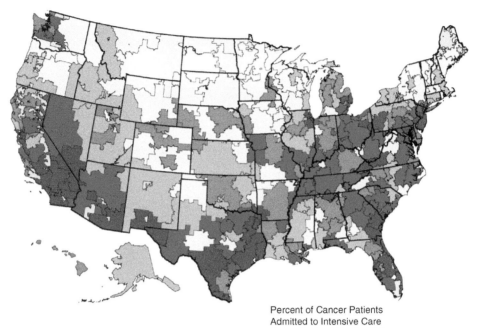

Percent of Cancer Patients
Admitted to Intensive Care
during the Last Month of Life
by HRR (deaths occuring 2003-07)

**Map 4. Percent of cancer patients admitted to intensive
care during the last month of
life (deaths occurring 2003-07)**

- 27% to 43% (62)
- 22% to <27% (64)
- 20% to <22% (57)
- 17% to <20% (58)
- 5% to <17% (65)
- Not populated

San Francisco   Chicago   New York   Washington-Baltimore   Detroit

A REPORT OF THE DART MOUTH ATLAS PROJECT 11

Source: The Dartmouth Institute: *The Dartmouth Atlas of Healthcare*

comprehensive information and analysis about national, regional, and local markets, as well as individual hospitals and their affiliated physicians.

Consider the map reproduced from the Dartmouth Atlas Report: "Quality of End-of-Life Cancer Care for Medicare Beneficiaries." It displays the percent of cancer patients admitted to intensive care during the last month of life compared by hospital referral regions. About 24% of cancer patients nationwide were admitted to intensive care at least once during that last month. However, the percent thus admitted varied more than sevenfold across those regions (dark red versus light yellow areas on the map). This map leads the viewer to ask, "Why are these rates so dramatically different across the country?," and perhaps to add an even more significant question: "What should the rate be?"

Geospatial displays of data like this one make the variation in end-of-life care jump off the page in a way that it never would if the data were buried in a table or report narrative. Such geospatial maps and accompanying reports, coupled with the underlying research, have helped policymakers, the media, healthcare analysts, and others improve their understanding of the efficiency and effectiveness of our healthcare system. As with the map created by John Snow, the visualizations built for the Dartmouth project make the story easy to see and understand and have formed the foundation for many of the nation's ongoing efforts to improve American health and healthcare systems.

Throughout history the power of data visualizations to help us see and consider the stories buried in our health and healthcare data has resulted in profound insights and often changes and improvement in our health and healthcare. And now with the advent of technology that allows us to amass data and quickly explore it, we are on the cusp of revolutionary insights and improvements. It is an exciting time indeed.

Chapter Two

Stop Hunting Unicorns and Start Building Teams and Know The Data

People often ask us what it takes to create clear and compelling displays of health and healthcare data that people love to use, and which raise awareness and move people to take action. The answer is paradoxically simple. It requires strong teams of experts in the highly complex disciplines of health and healthcare, statistics, data, technology, accessibility design, data visualization, and user experience testing—teams who appreciate the unique skills, experiences, and expertise each person brings to a project and the ability to work collaboratively.

Because here is the secret you already know. The idea that any lone person will ever have every single bit of expert knowledge and skill in health and healthcare, technical applications, and data visualization and design required to deliver beautiful and compelling dashboards, reports, and infographics is sheer lunacy. That's why organizations have to stop hunting unicorns and commit to building diverse teams who bring the expertise required and the ability to communicate and collaborate.

With that in mind, here is a summary of tips for building great data-analytics, reporting, and data visualization teams.

Search for Characteristics and Core Competencies

It is imperative to understand what characteristics and core competencies are required to complete the work. Here's where to begin:

Curiosity. When teams are curious, they question, probe, and inquire. Curiosity is a crucial impetus for uncovering interesting and relevant stories in our health and healthcare data. Above all else you need a team of really, genuinely inexhaustibly curious people!

Health and Healthcare Subject-Matter Expertise. Team members with front-line, boots-on-the-ground, clinical, quality, operational, policy, financial, research, and public health experience and expertise are essential for identifying the questions of interest and the decisions or needs of the stakeholders for and to whom data is being analyzed and communicated.

Data Analysis and Reporting. Without exception, at least one member of your team must have math, statistics, and data-analysis skills. Experience with data modeling is a plus if you can find it; at a minimum, some familiarity with the concept of modeling is beneficial. The ability to use data analysis, reporting, and display tools and applications is also highly desirable, but another more technically trained IT team member may be able to bring this ability to the table if necessary.

Technical: IT and Database Expertise. Often, groups will confuse this skill area with data-analysis and reporting competence.

Data and database architecture and administration require an entirely different set of skills from those needed for data analysis, so it's important not to conflate the two. You'll need team members who know how to extract, load, and transform (ETL) and architect data for analysts to use. And while you may sometimes find candidates who have both skill sets, don't assume that the presence of one means a lock on the other.

Data Visualization, Accessibility, and User Experience Testing. Knowledge of best practices and awareness of current research is required to create clear, useful, and compelling dashboards, reports, and infographics. But as you will learn in this book, these skills are not intuitive; they are based on research into human vision and cognition and must be learned and honed over time. And although it's not necessary for every team member to become an expert in this field, each should have some awareness of it to avoid working at cross-purposes with team members employing those best practices. (That is, everyone should know better than to ask for 3-D red, yellow, and green pie charts and other do's and don'ts you will learn in this book!)

We do wish that data-analysis and reporting unicorns were real! Life would be so much simpler. But they aren't and never will be, so we let go of that fantasy long ago and have found tremendous success in training and building great teams with the different skills that are required. We encourage you to do the same.

Get to Know the Data

The term *data governance* has become pervasive in the health and healthcare data environment. However, at present, any efforts at creating full-fledged data governance standards and associated documentation are at best nascent and more often nonexistent. Therefore, to perform correct analysis and create useful displays of data, analysts and data visualizers must establish discipline and process to learn and understand—and get to know—health and healthcare data.

Classifications, Intent, Purpose, and Lineage

Powerful data analysis and visualizations require subject-matter expertise about health and healthcare, and knowledge and understanding about the data being captured and reported. Whether it is a survey instrument, electronic health record, billing system, or the classification systems used to organize them and the databases to store them, diligent inquiry and research must be performed to ensure that the available data are fully understood. This discovery includes but is not limited to learning:

- How the data are categorized (classified) and relate to each other.
- Whether the data are part of a widely recognized and accepted classification system such as ICD10 Codes or a custom, unique system created for one particular project.
- Why, for what intent and purpose, a set of data is collected in the first place, such as medical claim payment, clinical research, patient care, public health initiatives.
- Moreover, and as necessary, how the data may have changed over time, their lineage.
- What the data definitions are.

For example, the HEDIS measure set was created in 1991 (version 1) and originally stood for the Health Maintenance Organization (HMO) Employer Data and Information Set. In 1994 version 2 was renamed the Health Plan Employer Data and Information Set. In the original design, HEDIS measures provided consumers and regulators with information to reliably compare competing managed care health plans. The focus was on how they were paying out premium dollars to providers for services. HEDIS was a marketing tool for HMOs to demonstrate that they were providing the most benefit to subscribers as compared to all other HMO plans.

A fundamental change occurred in 1997 when the National Committee for Quality Assurance (NCQA) adopted the HEDIS measure set as a way to measure and report about Medicare beneficiaries' quality of care. That is, the type of services delivered to specific cohorts of patients, such as mammograms for women, were used as proxies for quality care. At the same time, the NCQA also announced that the HEDIS acronym would be changed to stand for Healthcare Effectiveness Data and Information Set. Commercial insurers quickly followed suit, using HEDIS compliance targets in contract and payment negotiations with providers.

In some ways, it may be logical to use the HEDIS measure set as a proxy for the quality of care provided. For example, if the evidence supports that women of a certain age would benefit from an annual mammogram, and the number of eligible women receiving them can be reliably measured, then it may be that providing a mammogram is a reasonable proxy for quality care. However, as anyone who works in the health and healthcare profession knows, HEDIS falls short as a comprehensive measure of quality care because it does not capture the various outcomes that are important to clinicians, patients, researchers, and payers.

In other words, WYSIWYG (what you see is what you get) does not always (or even usually) apply to health and healthcare data. Therefore, it is crucial to take time to research the structure and categories of classification systems, and the primary purpose of a dataset, and how it may or may not be able to be reliably used for analysis and reporting.

Deciding on a set of terms (terminology) that accurately represent a system of concepts, creating a vocabulary with definitions of those terms, and arranging and organizing related entities into a classification system or database would appear to be a fairly straightforward (if long and detailed) task. Well, as the old joke goes, if you want 12 different opinions, put six people in a room and go around twice. (If they are experts in the field, the total will be closer to 24 different opinions.) Reaching consensus on how to define and classify health and healthcare information is tough. Evidence changes; treatments, procedures, and patients metamorphose; stakeholders define terms differently based on ever-shifting goals and objectives.

All these transformations mean that teams must dedicate time to research and consider the underlying classification systems of data definitions, and the intent, purpose, and lineage of health and healthcare databases. Starting here will save much frustration and wasted time later on and increase confidence about the ability to create valuable dashboards, reports, infographics, and other displays of health and healthcare data.

In addition to understanding the intent, purpose, and lineage of health and healthcare data, a fundamental understanding of data types, scales/levels of measure, and data relationships is required to create meaningful displays of data.

There is a wealth of books, publications, and blog postings on this topic, written by experts in the field of statistics and data analysis. The objective is not to recreate that level of detail here. Instead, the intention is to define and describe the data concepts that must be understood to ensure they are displayed correctly.

Two Types of Data

Qualitative/Categorical Data

Qualitative/categorical data are most easily understood as non-numerical data that may be observed but not measured or have mathematical functions performed on them, like a sum or average. Some examples may include a patient's eye color, sex, and perceptions about their health status or quality of care they received. Other examples may include measuring organizational change or physicians' implementation of evidence-based guidelines.

Sometimes these data are also described as *yes/no* data. For example, do people have food allergies, wear their seatbelt, smoke cigarettes, feel safe at home?

Although qualitative/categorical data can be coded with numerical values (e.g., 1 = male, 2 = female), those values do not have any mathematical meaning.

Quantitative/Numerical Data

Quantitative/numerical data measure the quantity or amount of something, and they are numerical, that is, they can be mathematically quantified and allow for the calculation of metrics such as sum, average. Quantitative/numerical data fall into one of two categories: continuous or discrete.

- Continuous data have an infinite number of possible values within a selected range, such as a patient's age, height, weight, blood sugar levels (A1C), pulse rate, respiratory rate.
- Discrete data items can be counted and have a finite number of possible values that can be listed out, such as prescriptions filled, hospital admissions, patients with diabetes, hours of exercise per week.

Scales/Levels of Measure

In the 1940s psychologist Stanley Smith Stevens introduced four scales, or levels of variable measurement: nominal, ordinal, interval, and ratio. Although not all data fall neatly into one of these four scales/levels (some examples follow), they are still widely used today. Foundational knowledge about them and the relationships they convey in health and healthcare data is key to creating well-designed tables and graphs.

Nominal

Nominal data are qualitative/categorical. These data may be most natural to remember as being "in name only." The reason for this is because there is no underlying prescribed order to them; no measure of the distance between values and categories can be listed in any order without affecting the relationship between them. It is merely a grouping of the data as a way to organize them, such as by race and ethnicity, language, country, state, department, clinical service, educational degrees, blood type, insurance type.

A famous and profound example of the power of carefully considering the arrangement of nominal data may be observed in the Vietnam Veterans Memorial in Washington, D.C. There are more than 58,000 names engraved on panels of polished black granite commemorating the Americans who died or were listed as Missing in Action (MIA) in the war. The obvious (and perhaps most neutral) way to list the names would have been alphabetically by the last name. Instead, designer Maya Ying Lin chose to list them chronologically *by date of death (or day reported missing).*

Ordering the soldiers by date of death serves to place them near one another as they may have fallen on the battlefield. It helps other soldiers who served at the same time to remember those whose deaths occurred during their tour of duty. It encourages visitors to contemplate the sacrifice of each soldier and to wonder at the connection of other visitors to the memorial. The simple, beautiful, and brilliant design of this memorial is something quite extraordinary in its dignified and engaging presentation of seemingly straightforward nominal data—the names of soldiers.

The Vietnam Veterans Memorial is a profound example of meaningful data visualization, and of the importance of design in communicating the message in our data. Alphabetically, the names are just that—data. When listed chronologically, as here, the same information tells a profoundly moving story.

DISPLAY TIP:

Nominal data may be displayed in any order, such as random, alphabetic, rank, or custom for an organization or defined project. What is paramount is the determination of the optimal arrangement that will convey the key message in the data and engage the viewer.

Ordinal

Ordinal data are qualitative/categorical. Ordinal relationships in data are characterized as having some underlying, meaningful order or sequence, although the intervals between scale points may be uneven. Some examples include academic achievement (High School, College, Graduate School), The American Society of

Anesthesiologist (ASA) Physical Classifications (1, 2, 3, 4, 5, 6), The Consumer Assessment of Healthcare Providers and Systems Survey (CAHPS) response categories (Never, Sometimes, Usually, Always), cancer staging (I, II, III, IV).

A special note of exception. Although months have a chronological order, January, February, March (through to December), and the intervals (days) between them are uneven, they are nevertheless treated as equal and included in the interval measure level.

DISPLAY TIP:

Never rank, alphabetize, or randomly display ordinal data. To display ordinal data out of their assigned order would not make sense, and may even cause viewers who are accustomed to seeing these data in their assigned order to miss something important or to draw incorrect conclusions. There may, however, be occasions when to convey the desired message *reversing the order* may make sense (for example, on CAHPS survey listing Always first, followed by Usually, Sometimes, and Never).

Interval

Interval data are quantitative/numerical. These data are ones in which we can make arithmetic assumptions about the degree of difference between values on a scale. For example, data is—or can be—divided into intervals (sometimes called bins) such as age ranges (20–29, 30–39, 40–49) or day ranges (0–5, 6–10, 11–15). Interval data have constant, equal distances between values, but the starting point is arbitrary.

As explained in the ordinal section above, although months have an uneven number of days, they are to be treated as though each month is equal and included in the interval measure level. Unlike nominal and ordinal data, meaningful mathematical comparisons can be made with interval data.

One special note of caution about Likert scales (e.g., with labels such as 1 = strongly disagree, 2 = disagree, 3 = neutral, 4 = agree and 5 = strongly agree). Sometimes researchers and analysts may be tempted to treat these as interval data, but that assumes that the differences between the points of the scale are equal. For example, the difference between strongly agree and agree is the same relative difference as between neutral and agree. However, careful consideration of this assumption makes it evident that it is unlikely to be true. For this reason, treat data captured using a Likert scale as ordinal data.

DISPLAY TIP:

Interval data is often displayed in a vertical bar graph called a histogram. A histogram helps viewers to see the distribution of the data along a scale, in the different intervals (bins), and whether they may be skewed or normally distributed. However, be careful to avoid the "My Bin or Yours?" and the "Different Bin Size" traps that are described in detail in Chapter 6. Histograms are not the only option, however. Month data may be displayed with different graph types such as a line or bar or a heat map, and all data may, of course, be displayed in a table.

Ratio

Ratio data are quantitative/numerical. Ratio scales have equal intervals between values, and they include a true zero point. (The inclusion of a true zero is essential because it allows for a meaningful ratio to be calculated, hence its name.) A few examples of ratio data include medication dose amount, lab values, pulse rate, respiratory rate, body temperature, and weight. For example, weight is ratio data because an infant can double its weight from 8 to 16 pounds or 16 to 32 pounds.

> **DISPLAY TIP:**
>
> It is important to remember that a true zero point is an actual value that imparts information to the viewer of tables and graphs and should be displayed as such.

Summary

This primer about the different types of data and levels of measure/scales is simply an introduction. Starting work with real health and healthcare data will reveal that not everything will fit neatly into one category. There will be different situations when the same data can be considered to have different levels of measure. When these times arise, discussion and study will need to occur to make sure the correct categorization and subsequent displays of the data are correct for the circumstances.

Chapter Three

Requirements-Gathering and Design Methods

Approaching a data visualization project can feel like being trapped in a carnival house of mirrors—those maze-like puzzles that are designed to confuse people in unusual, humorous, sometimes frightening, even paralyzing ways that visually distort and cloak the unobstructed path through and out.

But creating data visualizations does not have to feel that way. Establishing a process grounded in user-centered requirements-gathering and design thinking concepts and methods helps illuminate the path toward useful, understandable, visually pleasing data displays.

Design Thinking Foundational Concepts

Design thinking is a process for creative problem-solving that is human-centered, empathetic, collaborative, experimental, and optimistic. The process is not linear, but usually includes these five steps:

1. **Empathize.** Take the time and make the effort to learn about and empathize with the people for whom a data display is being created. To be effective, the designer must on some level recognize what clients and end-users experience—how they complete their work and tasks; their actions, interactions, decision patterns, and routines.

2. **Define.** Seek informative and compelling insights in order to define the problem, challenge, or objective that a data display is intended to solve. This may include information about a person's scope and role or responsibilities within an organization: decisions needed; tasks to accomplish; pressing issues to address.

3. **Ideate.** Generate several different potential approaches and solutions to a project. Adopt simple, participatory, human-centered design techniques, like brainstorming and collaborative sketching with designers, clients, and users to explore and discover unexpected and sometimes radical solutions to data and design challenges.

4. **Prototype.** Pilot ideas before fully implementing them. This allows for quick and low-cost failure by filtering out nonviable ideas early. The first low-fidelity prototyping is achieved through techniques like sketching. The second, higher-fidelity prototypes more closely resemble the final design in look and feel and sometimes even in basic functionality.

5. **Test.** Test ideas with stakeholders and/or people external to the project. This will lead to refinement of concepts and a more in-depth understanding of the user's needs and desires. Testing can reveal whether the selected data and design solution solves the original problem and conveys the intended message clearly; it can also uncover any needed modifications.

Design Methods

As described in Chapter 2, it truly does require a team with various skills and expertise to design, develop, and deploy dashboards, reports, or infographics with complex health and healthcare data. Integral to this effort is a conversation. Talking seems straightforward—something most of us can do—but facilitating and capturing the right information from the right people at the right time requires using established methods and techniques. The following are a few relatively simple strategies that, when used with conviction, are extraordinarily helpful.

Contextual Inquiry

Contextual inquiry places designers in the same environment and situations as the people they are designing for, allowing them to gain a new perspective through active observation and engage and inquire about the work and tasks as they are happening.

Four principles define the Contextual Inquiry method (Martin and Hanington, 2012, 46) and are especially helpful in developing dashboards and reports to support people in their day-to-day work:

- **Context.** Research underlying work structures in order to understand users' "ongoing experience" instead of just their "summary experience."
- **Partnership.** Spend time watching and participating in the work that people do to more thoroughly understand it. For example, watch how a scheduling office assigns patient appointments or surgical block time, or how community-based organizers search for data and information about the health of different communities. Participate in quality improvement team meetings or education initiatives. Observe the steps researchers go through to identify patient cohorts.
- **Interpretation.** Communicate observations back to the client or user to ensure that nothing has been misinterpreted, misunderstood, overlooked, or lost.

- **Focus.** Use the knowledge and insights gained about the user's world to expand initial focus and readjust approaches and solutions as needed.

Mental Models

Mental models are an explanation of a person's thought process about how something works in the real world. Understanding mental models can make it easier to construct a practical approach to solving problems and accomplishing tasks.

For example, consider how people read (in many, though not all, languages and cultures) a printed book. Often, they look at the Table of Contents first, then turn the book's pages from the right. They read the words on the pages from left to right, line by line, and from the first line at the top of the page to the last line at the bottom. If a passage holds particular interest, they may underline or highlight it, and if they come across an unfamiliar word, they sometimes look it up in a dictionary. (The process of reading a book, manuscript, or scroll in certain cultures may go in different directions—in columns, for example, or from the back of the book to the front—but comparable protocols are observed.)

Now think about the experience of reading a book on a Kindle or other electronic device. The contents of an e-book are arranged in the same order as in a printed one, and text is read from left to right and top to bottom. Moreover, some print activities are made more accessible in the electronic format: a word may be looked up in a built-in dictionary by merely touching it on the screen. The screen lights up in the dark so it can be read easily in bed or on a late-night flight. New books can be searched and downloaded directly from the device, including books from the local library.

Next, imagine how unsuccessful the developers of the Kindle would have been had they created an e-reader that required people to process a book in an entirely new and counterintuitive way—for example, by starting on the last page and reading from bottom to top and right to left. Furthermore, with no new or reimagined, easy-to-use functionality that made other tasks associated with books easier or better, how many people would have even considered reading on a Kindle? We are pretty sure the answer is very few.

This example makes it clear that it is tough, if not impossible, to get people to change the way they think about (that is, their mental model for thinking about) doing something simple, basic, and familiar—especially when that way or model works for almost everyone. In other words, if the potential audience for a visualization has a mental model for using data and information to support its work, that model must be revealed, understood, and built on to create something of value—visualizations that people will love to use and that will serve them well.

Useful questions for revealing and understanding mental models may include:

- What data does a user expect and want to see first on a dashboard?
- When users see a key indicator that requires further inquiry, what additional data do they expect/want to see next?
- Where do they expect different hyperlinks to go?
- Can you tell me the story of how you used data to solve a problem or complete a task, walking me through that process step by step?

Before ever sitting down to design data displays at a computer screen, a designer must learn as thoroughly as possible the process by which the intended audience uses the data to make decisions. Additionally, designers need to research the way users expect to navigate and interact with the final product based on their mental models about how something currently works and how they accomplish things. Furthermore, whenever possible, it's vital to come up with ways to improve the entire experience.

Personas

Personas are fictitious yet realistic users intended to help visualization designers remember the needs of the people for whom they conceive and construct reports, dashboards, and user interactions.

To create effective personas, designers should:

- Base them on solid research, using interviews and discussions to fully explore projected problem(s) or goal(s). Personas should not spring from the imagination; they need to take form and substance from specific traits and ideas gathered from real members of the client's staff or stakeholders.
- Be able to list concrete, tangible goals and problems to solve and—most important—how data displays will actually move people toward those goals and address those problems.
- Refer often to the personas they've created: draw up one-page profiles of them, with names, histories, and education; jobs, likes, and dislikes. Include a representative photo. Refer to these profiles often—consider them part of the team.
- As designs are discussed, ask questions out loud: How does this help the persona Jill? How will Jill use this? What does she need? How would she like to interact with the design, and when she does, will she call its elements and features useful tools, or distracting clutter that keeps her from doing her job?

Used correctly, personas help:

- Steer designers away from self-referential thinking, and keep them focused on the people for whom they are designing.
- Keep teams focused. Thanks to the immediacy and humanness of personas, instead of continually referring to anonymous "users," team members connect to realistic personalities in their projected audience. They stay focused on what can be done to make those people's lives easier, and concentrate on an important topic, not on which fancy chart they can create.

- Keep designs consistent, responsive, and needs appropriate. Personas help align designs with goals; data-display creators can return to them as to a touchstone to seek context, perspective, and reassurance that they are on the right track for a particular group of clients.
- Stay grounded in the core inquiries: Is this what the user needs most? Will this feature or design element make her day more manageable, her goals more reachable, her patients or her colleagues more comfortable, less stressed, more efficient, happier?

Personas are especially helpful when designing for multiple users who do similar work—for example, outpatient clinic managers or community-based organizers. Researching these similarities highlights commonalities that can be used to create a persona that represents them as a group. Creating personas will result in a design that meets many of their common needs, thereby avoiding the "700 flavors of vanilla" phenomenon that often results from trying to serve all users with similar objectives and tasks, but slightly nuanced individual requests.

Persona Creation Guide

FIGURE 3.1 Personas help designers remember the needs of the people for whom they are creating displays of data.

Name. Give personas names to make them feel more real. Refer to them by name as a project develops.

Photos. Sometimes it is also helpful to use a stock photo to bring a persona to life and make them seem like part of the team.

Age. May be of help, especially if the project is focused on providing information to a public that consists of, for example, older/elderly audiences versus teenagers.

Education. Level of education (MD, PhD, BSN, MPH, high school diploma) may provide some insights into a persona's level of expertise and experience in a field.

Years in Position. Knowing how long someone has held a position in an organization may establish her/his level of expertise.

Scope of Responsibility/Role in an Organization or Other Group Such as a Family. Job titles or roles in the family may be of some help here, but they are not enough. Specific information gathered through research about what people are responsible for (e.g., an entire organization, one department, one project, finances, safety, clinical care, seeking care for a family member) and what they do for work or in the group (e.g., ensuring patients are scheduled in a timely way, quality benchmarks are being met, public health warnings are being disseminated; providing daily care for a disabled child) is required. Dig in to learn and document the details.

Decisions. What decisions does the persona need to make within its scope and role? The data and information included in displays must be able to inform and support these decisions.

Outcomes. For infographics, what is the desired outcome? Is it to raise awareness, teach, persuade, and move viewers to action?

Familiarity/Experience with Data and Statistics. The persona's level of experience and expertise will help to inform the level of complexity that may be required to be displayed, and the explanatory/helper text accompanying them. Inclusion of statistical significance is important to researchers, but may not be required for the general public viewing an infographic of data curated by experts.

Access to Data Displays. How will the persona access the data displays? On an interactive website portal, mobile device? A slide deck, printed report? Will they use a screen reader? All of these? This information will ensure that designs are optimized for different formats.

Frustrations. Through research, frustrations will be revealed. Include them in personas to serve as a reminder about what can be improved and what problems need to be solved.

Quotations. Often a single quotation captured during the research will help to illuminate the goals and objectives of a project.

Graphic Organizers

Group sessions, where lots of new ideas are generated rapidly and without judgment, have been used in all types of design projects for decades. More recently, the use of graphic organizers or visual representations of knowledge has been introduced to support teams as they challenge assumptions and search for the best solutions. For health and healthcare data visualization projects, these graphic organizers provide a framework to map out and consider data hierarchies, organizational hierarchies (including users' scope, role, and responsibilities), or the component parts of important health and healthcare topics. They offer teams a structure for the process of puzzling out together the required data and layout for dashboards, reports, and infographics.

Guided Analytics Framework

A diagram like the one in Figure 3.2 illustrating the concept of Guided Analytics is invaluable when figuring out together how to display masses of complex data for management and business reporting (for example). Coupled with research and knowledge about an organization's management reporting structure, users' roles and responsibilities within that structure, their decision patterns and routines, and data categories and hierarchies, it helps teams map where indicators should be logically displayed.

In the Guided Analytics Framework diagram in Figure 3.2, the highest level displays an executive summary of key indicators. The next level includes more data and contextual information about the different categories/indicators shown at the executive summary level, but presented in individual focused reports. Detailed supporting data is then available in the form of lists and tables. Analysts and managers who have the knowledge and need to consider the data through multiple lenses may have specially designed views with many interactive filters and capabilities.

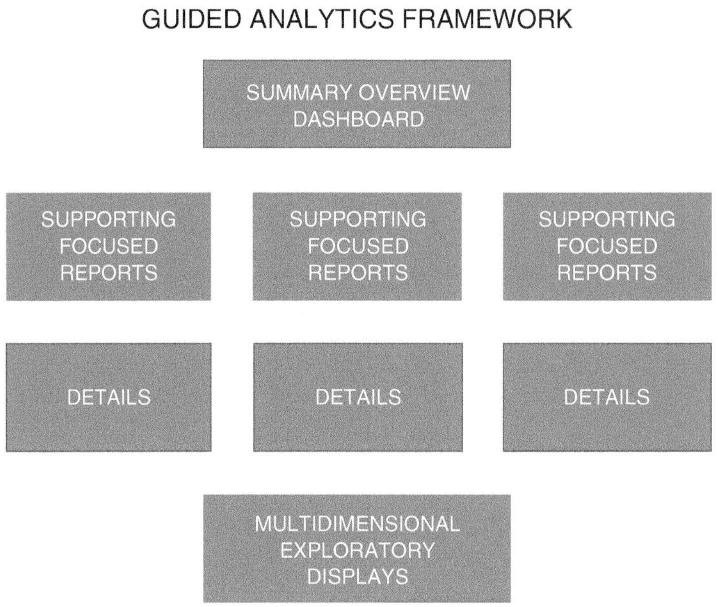

GUIDED ANALYTICS FRAMEWORK

FIGURE 3.2   Guided analytics framework.

Summary Overview Dashboard

- **Data.** Concise summaries of key and comparison metrics.
- **Design Characteristics/Functionality.** Fits on one page or screen in a predetermined format. Electronic versions have few or no user selections for a low "click burden."

Supporting Focused Reports

- **Data.** Expanded data about a category, topic, or key metric.

- **Design Characteristics/Functionality.** May be on one or more pages or scrolling in a predetermined format. Electronic versions have more selection choices to sort and filter the data. Allows for more and different views, higher click burden (e.g., by region, department, patient cohort, or date).

Details

- **Data.** Underlying details such as patients, providers, survey respondents, charges, prescriptions by name, labs by test type.
- **Design Characteristics/Functionality.** Usually lists and sometimes tables of detailed data. Electronic versions have extensive functionality to select the data to be listed with high click burden.

Multidimensional Exploratory Displays (MEDs™)

- **Data.** Extensive access to underlying data for exploration.
- **Design Characteristics/Functionality.** May have a consistently formatted layout or may be user defined depending on the design of the application. Designed for expert users to explore the data and has the highest click burden to generate different displays of data.

A Guided Analytics approach need not follow this exact model and content, but will always guide a user through data, starting with high-level summary metrics and providing access to increasingly focused and detailed data displays specific to metrics or associations of interest to the user.

★★★

Refer to Chapter 10 to learn more about dashboards, reports, and MEDs™ design. Graphic organizers are also invaluable in the development of infographics. Refer to Chapter 11 for more details on how they may be used to establish a hierarchy in the planning stage, identify the main components of the story, and define how those components will be sequenced on the page or screen.

PROCESS TIP:

Do not worry about what type of graphs to use at this stage of the process. Focus on the indicators to be displayed, the comparisons to be used (budget, benchmark, goal, national averages), and other contextual information such as the time-frames (week, month, year) and narratives to be included. Once these are defined, choices concerning graphs and design tradeoffs will be much clearer and easier. Determining, in short, *what* will be displayed will inform the best practice of *how* to display it.

Sketching

Sketching is a fast, easy, collaborative, and low-cost way to generate lots of ideas and possible solutions. It also connects participants to the creative process differently from the way that software applications can.

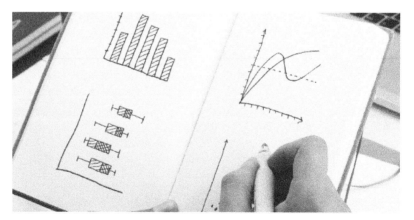

FIGURE 3.3 Sketching is a low-cost, low-risk, quick-and-easy way to experiment with possible layouts and solutions.
Source: Peter Massarelli

- Sketching is useful to display or illustrate things such as spatial relationships and graphical layouts that can be hard to describe in words.

- Done in groups, it allows for the collaborative exploration of ideas and of unconventional, even potentially radical solutions to problems.

- Sketching frees groups to experiment in a very low-cost, low-risk, quick-and-easy way: there is no pressure or requirement to "get it right."

- As compared with hours spent trying to perfect early designs using a software application, paper sketches rarely leave behind hurt feelings and frustration when they are crumpled up and tossed away.

Sketching may be accomplished in simple ways, using markers and paper, sticky notes, or a whiteboard. Groups can be split into teams to develop ideas, then come together to compare and consolidate. The value of sketching throughout the research and initial design sessions must not be dismissed. Instead, sketching must become an integral and fun part of the process.

Prototyping

Prototyping allows teams to fail quickly and cheaply by piloting ideas before fully implementing them. The first type, low-fidelity prototyping, is achieved through techniques like sketching described above. There is no need to wrangle actual data into shape and no investment of hours spent staring at a computer screen trying to get every pixel precisely right. The process is fast and financially and emotionally cheap.

The second type is high-fidelity prototypes. Best developed using a small extract of representative data to create displays, these prototypes more closely resemble the final design in look and feel and sometimes even in basic functionality.

Using this second type provides users with dashboards, reports, and infographics that more closely resemble the finished product and that provide feedback to designers and developers.

> ## TIP:
>
> *Never* send out high-fidelity prototypes to users "cold" and request "feedback." This is a sure path to disaster and frustration for everyone. Explain to users up front that prototypes will never be distributed without the designer's first having an opportunity to show and explain them. This small but essential and disciplined step in the design process provides designers and developers the opportunity to:
>
> - Explain the design approach and any tradeoffs that had to be made due to problems with the underlying data or limits of software applications.
> - Show users (and familiarize them with) interactive functionality.
> - Hear and respond to first reactions.
> - Make any modifications before giving the prototype to users for a tryout and the generation of additional feedback.
>
> Failure to implement this step in the process will very often result in frustrated users who feel that they have not been heard or understood; further (and worse) it may jeopardize a project and demoralize teams.

Testing

Here are a couple of straightforward and inexpensive ways to test dashboards, reports, and infographics. Using the figures and graphs as your guide, practice speaking out loud (yes, out loud) to test if you can create a cohesive, fluent, and compelling narrative.

If you are successful in telling a guided story about the data and information on the reports and dashboards before you, then it is highly likely the end-users will be able to as well. Conversely, if you find yourself struggling and stumbling to say what you see, then you know you probably need to refine or modify the design.

This method may not be easy. When you have to describe—in your own words, and verbally—what you have created clearly and compellingly, using detailed explanations with examples from the data, you may find it difficult, frustrating, even a little scary.

Keep at it; in the long run, you will discover that it helps you create much more comprehensive and effective reports and dashboards.

Another practical and straightforward approach to testing dashboards, reports, and infographics is to draft about three or four precise questions that you believe users should be able to answer when viewing the data display. Tailor the questions specifically to the data displayed. For example:

- What was the rate of teenage pregnancies in North Dakota in 2018?
- How many readmissions did Memorial Hospital have in December? Which department had the highest number?
- What was the average age of Medicaid beneficiaries in the United States five years ago?
- Is the difference between the number of teenagers in Community A reporting that they smoke cigarettes and the same number in Community B statistically significant?

Provide several users with the data display and the questions, then simply observe how easily they find the answers. Do not coach or help. If they all struggle with answering the questions in the same places, that offers valuable insight into where the design should be improved.

Testing need not be elaborate or expensive, but it must be done to ensure that dashboards, reports, infographics, and exploratory tools are adopted and used.

Summary

Establishing a process grounded in user-centered design thinking concepts and methods reduces the time, cost, frustration, and discarded solutions that occur when organizations believe that staff members should intuitively "know what is needed and build it."

Perceiving the Best Practices of Data Visualization

"No matter how clever the choice of information, and no matter how technologically impressive the encoding, a visualization fails if the decoding fails. Some display methods lead to efficient, accurate decoding, and others lead to inefficient, inaccurate decoding. It is only through scientific study of visual perception that informed judgements can be made about display methods."

—William S. Cleveland,
The Elements of Graphing

Chapter Four

The Research

Research Informs Data Visualization Best Practices

Data visualization relies on visual perception and interpretation, so understanding how and why humans see and perceive what they do is crucial to creating engaging, accurate, and meaningful data displays.

As Colin Ware, author of *Information Visualization: Perception for Design*, writes:

> The human visual system is a pattern seeker of enormous power and subtlety … [that] has its own rules. We can easily see patterns presented in certain ways, but if they are presented in other ways, they become invisible. … Following perception-based rules, we can present our data in such a way that the important and informative patterns stand out. If we disobey the rules, our data will be incomprehensible or misleading. (Ware, 2020, xiv)

It, therefore, follows that learning visualization techniques grounded in research on human cognition and vision are essential to ensuring that the most important patterns, trends, and variances—the vital message and stories in health and healthcare data—are easy to perceive and understand.

Additionally, the abundance of stimuli continually bombarding us means that now, more than ever, data visualizers must study and understand the existing and emerging research about how the human brain processes visual information, and how the results of this research inform the best practices of data visualization. The window to get and retain attention for the important stories, and opportunities to learn and improve health and healthcare systems, is narrow and the competition for attention stiff.

How stiff? Research has found that thanks to the growing presence of digital media in our lives, our attention span has declined from 12 seconds (in 2000) to about 8 seconds (2013). Sadly, at 9 seconds, the attention span of a goldfish is now longer than ours. (See Figure 4.1.)

GOLDFISH HAVE A LONGER ATTENTION SPAN THAN HUMANS

AVERAGE HUMAN ATTENTION SPAN IN **2000**
12 seconds

AVERAGE HUMAN ATTENTION SPAN IN **2013**
8 seconds

GOLDFISH ATTENTION SPAN
9 SECONDS

Data Source: Microsoft Canada,
http://dl.motamem.org/microsoft-attention-spans-research-report.pdf | Visual: HDV

FIGURE 4.1 A drop in human attention span makes it imperative that data visualizers understand how research informs the best practices of data visualization.

Vision is the strongest of the five senses, accounting for 70% of how information is taken in and made sense of. However, the human brain is highly selective, processing only about 5% of what is transmitted to it through vision. These limits serve to help humans focus on critical tasks, whether instinctual or honed through training and experience and stored in memory. Seeing and knowing to pick the one ripe red apple on a tree of mostly unripened green ones, responding with caution to a dark shape moving on the periphery, or generating a fight-or-flight response to a deadly predator are all examples of how our vision and brain communicate and help us to navigate (and survive in) the world.

A less instinctual task—one that depends on previous training and experience stored in memory to make sense—is reading text. As you read this book, your eyes focus on groups of words, not individual letters. These words have been previously learned and stored in memory, thereby creating the mechanism for your brain to take a shortcut and transform them instantly into words you know and understand.

> For emaxlpe, it deson't mttaer in what oredr the ltteers in a wrod aepapr, as lnog as the frist and lsat ltteer are in the crocret pcale. The rset can be a toatl mses and you can sitll raed it. S1M1L4RLY, Y0UR M1ND 15 R34D1NG 7H15 4U70M471C4LLY W17H0U7 3V3N 7H1NK1NG 4B0U7 17.

In day-to-day interactions, many details (a room's wall color; the unique features of people passing by on the street) are not processed by the brain because they would overwhelm it. Processing everything that enters the line of vision makes it impossible to focus on any one thing (including the very important task of reading this book!).

Wired to select the most critical information, the human brain, through vision, pays attention to things that stand out or are different from their surroundings. It seeks patterns and variations, then stores them for use in identifying the same or similar information when it is reencountered.

Preattentive Attributes

Preattentive processing takes place at humans' lowest visual acuity, occurring in milliseconds and registering select signals before the conscious mind is fully aware of what is happening. During these milliseconds, the brain seeks out and pays attention to specific properties and patterns it registers as being different or critical.

In data visualization, this means viewers will instantaneously see specific visual cues designed to leverage attributes of preattentive processing. Adding these visual cues to data displays can be powerful tools for signaling "look here!" and, when used accurately, will result in immediate insight.

The three common preattentive attributes (Figure 4.2) in data visualization are:

- Color (hue, intensity)
- Form (size, orientation, shape)
- Spatial position (length, width, position)

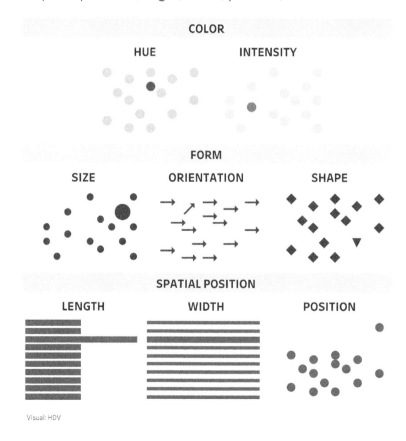

Visual: HDV

FIGURE 4.2   Examples of preattentive attributes.

Preattentive Attributes at Work

The following is an example of how preattentive processes work.

Look at the table in Figure 4.3. How quickly can you identify the state with the highest expense? The lowest expense? The top five states in both categories?

ALL PAYORS DRUGS & NON-DURABLE
2014 Annual Expenditures ($Millions)

Location	Per Capita Drugs & Non-Durable
Arizona	$5,467
Florida	$24,504
Georgia	$9,467
Kansas	$3,243
Massachusetts	$8,437
Michigan	$10,964
Minnesota	$5,206
Nevada	$2,736
New Jersey	$12,089
New York	$28,294
Ohio	$11,866
Oklahoma	$4,576
Oregon	$3,501
Pennsylvania	$17,208
South Carolina	$5,758

Data Source: CMS.gov - Health Expenditures by State of Residence, 1991-2014. Table 18. | Visual: HDV

FIGURE 4.3   Table listing annual expenditures.

Scanning a table of numbers and making comparisons requires much time and mental energy. Making multiple eye movements, reading each line, searching for patterns or specific values, and retaining a large amount of information in short-term memory needed to evaluate and compare values is hard and requires patience and focus. More often than not, viewers will simply give up. This difficulty comes from the fact that tables are designed for looking up and comparing individual, precise values, not for spotting patterns and trends.

If there is a need to direct a viewer's attention to specific values, such as their ranking, we can arrange and label the table in the desired order. However, if the need is to ensure that the viewers see a specific value immediately, then adding a preattentive attribute—a "look here" signal—is required.

In Figure 4.4, the addition of the color red in the table highlights the value with the lowest expenditures and immediately attracts the viewer's attention. It is almost impossible not to notice the red, bolded font, because it signals, "Look here! This value is important."

ALL PAYORS DRUGS & NON-DURABLE
2014 Annual Expenditures ($Millions)

Location	Per Capita Drugs & Non-Durable
Arizona	$5,467
Florida	$24,504
Georgia	$9,467
Kansas	$3,243
Massachusetts	$8,437
Michigan	$10,964
Minnesota	$5,206
Nevada	$2,736
New Jersey	$12,089
New York	$28,294
Ohio	$11,866
Oklahoma	$4,576
Oregon	$3,501
Pennsylvania	$17,208
South Carolina	$5,758

Data Source: CMS.gov - Health Expenditures by State of Residence, 1991-2014. Table 18. | Visual: HDV

FIGURE 4.4   Table using preattentive attribute (Color).

This "pop-out" effect is the result of preattentive processing—processing that occurs before our conscious, attentive mind kicks in.

These visual prompts are most effective when the differences are based on one element: size (big/small) or color (red/black). As stated previously, however, the human brain cannot take in everything, so preattentive attributes become less distinct as their use and variety increases. Ware (2004, 157) states that "it is easy to spot a single hawk in a sky full of pigeons, but if the sky contains a greater variety of birds, the hawk will be more difficult to see."

Figure 4.5 shows another preattentive example: length. Bar charts use length, or spatial position, to show values across a dimension, as length supports making quick visual comparisons.

In the following display, the eye is quickly drawn to the comparative lengths of the bars—particularly to the longest one. By adding color and sorting, we can direct attention and convey a clear story: "New York had the greatest health expenditures"; "Ohio is among the top five states in healthcare spending."

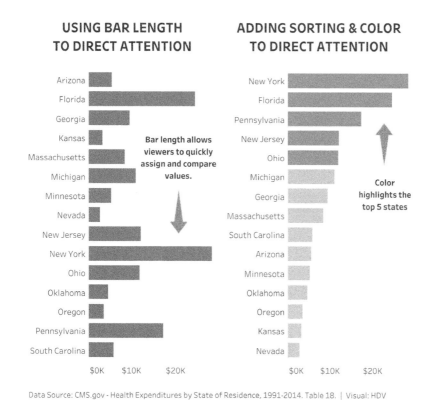

Data Source: CMS.gov - Health Expenditures by State of Residence, 1991-2014. Table 18. | Visual: HDV

FIGURE 4.5 Preattentive attribute of length in a bar chart.

Preattentive attributes can be used in data visualization to add context, frame a story, draw attention, or evoke emotion. They determine what we see first and pay the most attention to. Other visual principles guide how we organize and understand our visual world through patterns.

Gestalt Principles

Gestalt psychology is the study of visual perception, and of the laws and principles that guide how humans tend to search for patterns and organize visual elements into groups or unified wholes.

Understanding Gestalt principles helps inform the optimal arrangement of data on dashboards, reports, and infographics. Figure 4.6 shows several examples of Gestalt principles in a display of mock data.

Proximity. Objects arranged close together are perceived as a group. Shapes close to one another, such as different points or shape points on a scatterplot, appear to belong to groups, and each group is interpreted as having a common element or characteristic.

Similarity. Objects that share similar attributes, such as color, direction, or shape, are perceived as being part of a group. Using shapes to distinguish between two dimensions in one chart or color on a dashboard, such as male and female in Figure 4.6, can help the viewer more readily identify which groups the displayed data belong with.

Enclosure. Objects collected within a boundary-like structure are perceived as a group, so placing a line or shading around elements signals that objects within the boundary form one. In Figure 4.6, the box encloses all data related to one sex.

Connection. Connected objects are perceived as a group. For example, adding a line to a scatterplot helps us to determine if there is any relationship (connection/correlation) between variables. Using a line to connect time series data sends a signal to the viewer that the points are sequential and connected.

GESTALT PRINCIPLES

All rates are per 100,000 population.

Data Source: CDC; https://www.cdc.gov/nchs/data/hus/2018/fig03.pdf | Visual: HDV

FIGURE 4.6 Gestalt Principles.

Continuity. Objects aligned or in continuation of one another are perceived as a group, when in reality they are separated or interrupted. In the Gestalt dashboard in the figure, although the trendline has a break/gap to signal there is no data for the period, the tendency is to mentally complete the pattern to the end of the line.

Arranging data on dashboards, reports, and infographics in alignment with Gestalt principles will result in well-organized, unified displays. In them, viewers will be able to see how the data logically fit together, and to identify and consider potentially important relationships in the presentation. Failing to understand and leverage these principles will most often result in jumbled and disorganized displays that risk burying the lead in the data's story.

Color Theory

As in all art, color in data visualization must be used with intention and purpose, not arbitrarily. Each color choice should add value—not muddle a display, or overwhelm, confuse, or (even worse) mislead viewers. Color is a powerful tool that can aid in signaling an action, draw attention to crucial information, and, even evoke strong emotions. For example, the green light in a traffic signal indicates that vehicles may proceed through an intersection. The color yellow can influence mood by evoking warm, cheerful, energetic feelings, and even affect physiological reactions.

Depending upon the country or culture, the color red can signal vastly different messages: a warning of trouble or danger on the one hand, a symbol of wealth, prosperity, happiness, and good luck on the other. It is essential to consider the intended audience's experience and the context in which the color will be used in order to choose colors that will resonate and elicit the intended response.

Three components typically describe the visual nature of color (Figure 4.7): hue or color name, saturation or chroma, and lightness or value. Adjusting each of these components changes the overall perceptual impact of the color on the person viewing it. Because humans respond so strongly to colors, it is an important design element in data visualization.

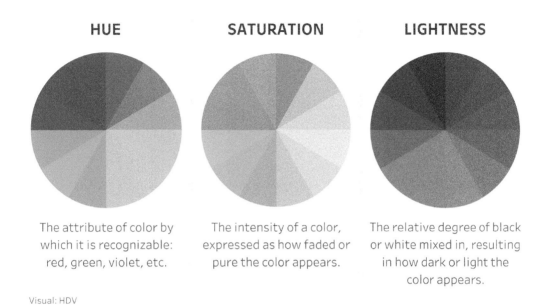

HUE	SATURATION	LIGHTNESS
The attribute of color by which it is recognizable: red, green, violet, etc.	The intensity of a color, expressed as how faded or pure the color appears.	The relative degree of black or white mixed in, resulting in how dark or light the color appears.

Visual: HDV

FIGURE 4.7   Three components of color.

Using each of these color attributes in different ways can help show data directly and clearly, drawing attention to its most crucial elements. Techniques such as the use of desaturated colors in part of the display can help "calm" the visual. For example, although often overlooked, the muted nature of the color gray can be beneficial when designing dashboards: it softens the overall view and allows other colors used to highlight trends, variances, and differences (the most critical data on the visual) to stand out.

It is also essential to consider where eliminating color can improve the overall display. Color must be used above all to highlight the data and draw attention to critical elements. Using a rainbow of colors indiscriminately will serve only to spoil visualizations and overwhelm and confuse viewers.

Color Gradients

Data visualization uses three main types of color gradients (Figure 4.8): sequential, diverging, and qualitative.

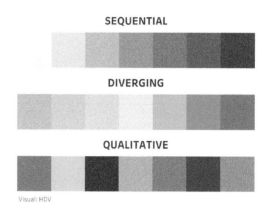

Visual: HDV

FIGURE 4.8   Three types of color gradients.

Sequential gradients use one color of different saturations to generate a scale that displays the lowest (least saturated) to the highest (most saturated) data values. These gradients should be used when there is no midpoint or value by which to compare numbers.

The map in Figure 4.9 shows the percentage of people reporting having coronary obstructive pulmonary disease (COPD) across various countries. Because there is no defined midpoint or target, a sequential palette is best for this display.

Diverging gradients use at least two distinct colors on each end of the value range being displayed, such as red/blue, yellow/purple, green/brown. Zero or some relevant comparison value should be represented by a third, neutral color (such as white or gray) midscale to make it clear when the two diverging colors shift from one value to another.

For example, in Figure 4.9, a calendar heatmap shows the average number of minutes a surgery lasted compared to the expected number. The colors indicate which days had an average of minutes above (green) or below (purple) the central or diverging point of zero.

Qualitative palettes use colors of varying hues and saturation, which can make them ideal for distinguishing between non-associated data values. Qualitative palettes must be used carefully: more than four or five different colors will become confusing and challenging to make sense of.

In Figure 4.9, the qualitative example of adolescent birthrates consists of four distinct colors of varying hues, each representing a different race.

It is important to note that legends, which can vary in design, are necessary for comprehending all displays that use gradient color-coding of data.

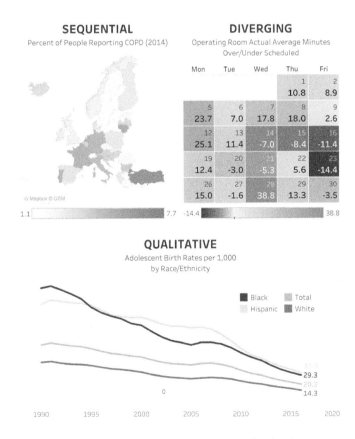

FIGURE 4.9   Color gradient examples.

Effective Use of Color

When selecting colors for data visualizations, consider appropriateness, aesthetics, and the emotions the colors may evoke. In certain circumstances, consider selecting colors that convey some additional emotion and meaning. For example, visualizations about the rates of lung cancer due to smoking; heart disease; or gangrene may be rendered strikingly effective through color selections that have been associated with each disease, and therefore evoke strong memories and emotions—for example, the colors orange for lung cancer, red for heart disease, and black for gangrene. While these are stark and sobering examples, they make it possible to dispassionately observe the connections between diseases and colors and the emotions they call up.

Another critical consideration in color selection is the fact that not all people see color the same way. Everyone has some differences in perception, especially of tertiary/intermediate colors (colors made by mixing full saturation of one primary color with half saturation of another primary color and none of a third primary color), so it is always important to test color selection via user feedback.

Further, it is estimated that 8% of men and .05% of women in the world are colorblind and unable to distinguish between certain colors—most commonly red and green. Colors and techniques (such as the use of different-shaped icons) that address this vision deficiency are covered in Chapter 9.

Color Summary

Keeping in mind the overall and specific objectives of a visualization, always consider how color can help achieve them. Use color to:

- Grab and hold attention.
- Show patterns and call attention to important variances and differences.
- Inspire a viewer to take action.
- Trigger a specific feeling or emotion.

Color Do's and Don'ts

DO NOT use color indiscriminately. It should be used purposefully in the service of the story, message, or data to be communicated.

DO limit visuals to three colors whenever possible to reduce color overload. Follow the 60-30-10 rule: 60% of color should be dominant, 30% a secondary color, and 10% the accent.

DO use one color (sequential) to represent continuous data, from lower values (less saturation) to higher values (more saturation). Use at least two colors (diverging) when there is a value from which to "diverge," such as zero or a specific target value.

DO use color judiciously to defend against boredom due to repeated viewing. Make sure that the important stories continue to shine through, and that colors serve that objective.

DO select colors that are accessible for viewers with visual impairments, such as colorblindness.

DO use color consistently. For example, if data about Drug A is displayed on two charts, do not make it blue on one and red on another.

DO incorporate an organization's brand colors (when required) appropriately, and without violating the best practices of data visualization or compromising the overall visualization.

The Power of White Space

White (also called negative) space has been described as "underrated as the silence between musical notes" (Soegaard, 2019). The area/space between core design elements, and the space between smaller design elements (often referred to as macro and micro white space), help organize and balance content. The power of white space is that it can help guide a viewer through a display, and serve as a calming element to help viewers "breathe" and not feel overwhelmed.

Where People Look

Eye-tracking research reveals that people typically view screens in an F-shaped pattern, working in a horizontal flow from left to right, then top to bottom, and covering less horizontal distance the further they get down the page. Similarly, when viewing a dashboard, people often look in this zigzag pattern from top left to top right, then bottom left to bottom right. Note that preattentive attributes may direct attention away from this pattern, but in general, the top-left corner of a dashboard is prime real estate. Therefore, that corner and the top first row of a dashboard should be reserved for the most important information to be conveyed. If a dashboard is arranged in columns, then the leftmost column of information, in a top-to-bottom order within it, will be viewed first before the other columns. The key takeaway is awareness of the space on a dashboard and where to place objects, graphs, and tables within it.

Grids and predesigned templates available in most software applications are an important aid in the placement of data and information to be displayed in/on a report, dashboard, infographic, print material, or web page. Using a specific template for a collection or series of displays provides a consistent view for users that helps them gain familiarity with the displays and reduces the amount of tiring switching or reorienting that can become necessary with multiple layouts. Grids and templates also make the designer/visualizer's work easier. They help keep displays organized and in alignment with what is known about where people look first on screens and dashboard data displays.

Summary

Understanding the research about how people perceive data and information through vision, and how that informs the best practices of data visualization, is foundational to designing clear, compelling, and actionable displays of data.

Chapter Five

Table Design Checklist

Fundamentals of Table Design

Tables are the most fundamental of display devices, arranging values in rows and columns in order to look up and compare specific, precise values. Ensuring that tables are well-designed and easy to use requires understanding the best practices of table design, detailed in the following checklists.

Organization/Categorization

- Simple lookups of data may be best organized alphabetically or numerically (for nominal data where there is no underlying order).
- Data that is part of an accepted/standardized taxonomy is best ordered in alignment with that system—for example, tumor classification or ICD10 hierarchy.
- Data may also be arranged to most effectively communicate the story, for example, by ranked results or areas requiring attention

(e.g., not meeting goal) versus tables designed to look up and compare values such as by geographic region or medical service.

- Calculated columns are arranged logically, reflecting how they were calculated. For example: numerator (column A) divided by denominator (column B) equals percentage or rate (column C); value (column A) minus value (column B) equals difference (column C).

Non-Data Ink

- Eliminate as much non-data ink (heavy gridlines, unnecessary colors) as possible to ensure the data is the star. Gridlines have been lightened or eliminated.
- White space or light highlighting is used to differentiate rows and columns of data.
- See Figure 5.1 for an example.
- Color-coding of cells to impart trends or some other pattern or meaning better communicated with a graph or heatmap table has been eliminated.
- Techniques, such as bolding or italics, to highlight relevant data have been used sparingly.

Fonts

- Use monospace (non-proportional) san-serif fonts like Consolas or Arial Unicode MS to ensure values have equal space on the page, and numbers in columns are aligned.
- Commas are used for numbers with more than three digits (e.g., 1,000).

Number Alignment and Formatting

- All numbers are right-justified to ensure values (e.g., ones, tens, hundreds, thousands) are aligned.
- Zeros are eliminated whenever possible (e.g., $1,000,000 displayed as $1M or highest values clearly noted in title or labels).

ROW BANDING
Use Light Shading to Guide Viewers' Eyes Across Rows

Group 1	500	525	575	600	625
Group 2	525	1,025	550	675	2,500
Group 3	550	725	1,700	1,200	685
Group 4	575	825	1,095	825	715
Group 5	4,000	925	475	900	745

WHITE SPACE
Use White Space to Differentiate Between Columns and Rows

Group 1	500	525	575	600	625
Group 2	525	1,025	550	675	2,500
Group 3	550	725	1,700	1,200	685
Group 4	575	825	1,095	825	715
Group 5	4,000	925	475	900	745

Mock Data | Visual: HDV

FIGURE 5.1 Reduce non-data ink and make data the focus.

- The level of precision matches the needs of the end-user. Numbers are included after a decimal point to add required precision only when required.
- Negative values are displayed with accepted standards, for example, parenthesis, minus sign, or colored in red: (65), –65, (–65), –65.

Labels

- Plain language is used to describe the table columns and rows. The writing is designed to ensure the reader understands what is being displayed quickly, easily, and thoroughly. Information about the values being displayed is included (e.g., dollars ($), percentage (%), count (#), days, hours, minutes).
- Date ranges of the data are included in heading and titles.
- Labels are nested to allow space for descriptions. Footnotes have been eliminated or significantly reduced, and summary calculations that help users understand the data are included as part of the labels wherever possible.
- If the table rows flow onto more than one page, column headers are repeated on each page.
- Labels are oriented horizontally.
- See Figure 5.2 for an example.

Number of Newly Diagnosed Cases of HIV - January 20xx
(<5 Cases Surpressed)

Region 1   Region 2   Region 3   Region 4

Mock Data | Visual: HDV

FIGURE 5.2   Summarize headings and orient them horizontally so they are easy to read.

Summary

Do not overlook the importance of the best practices when creating a table of data and information to ensure users can easily see, find, and compare values. Although seemingly simple, a well-designed table will ensure that users can access the information they need quickly and easily and without mistakes.

Chapter Six

Powerful Visualizations in Four Shapes

Bars, Lines, Points, and Boxes

It is incredible how many displays of data can be created using bars, lines, points, and boxes (alone and in combination) to create elegantly simple yet powerfully effective visualizations. In this chapter, we reveal how versatile these four fundamental shapes can be, and how to use them to display clear, actionable health and healthcare data by following best practices. (See Figure 6.1.)

Note: The term *chart* refers to a method for presenting information such as a table, a diagram, or a graph. Therefore, all graphs are charts but not all charts are graphs. In most places we have used the term *graph* for the mathematical relationship between sets of data, but in some places we use the term *chart* simply to make the narrative a bit more interesting.

The icons shown in Figure 6.2 have been included to indicate which graphs and charts to never use, or use with caution.

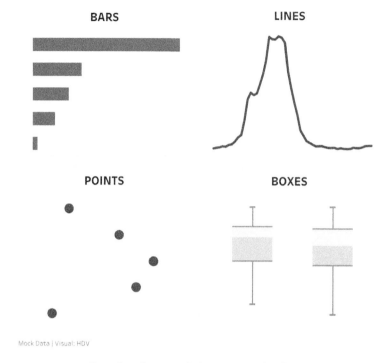

Mock Data | Visual: HDV

FIGURE 6.1   Four fundamental shapes are the foundation of great data visualizations.

| Never Use | Use With Caution | Best Practice |

FIGURE 6.2   Icons are used to indicate graphs and charts to never use, or use with caution, and the best practice choice.

Shape One: Bars

A true pillar of data visualization, bars display and compare values such as numbers, frequency, distribution, or statistical mean or median for different discrete categories of data. Bars order data by ranking or help us to see and comprehend the distribution of a dataset, such as whether it is skewed to the left or right or is normally distributed. Bars can show deviation (change) from a baseline or target, and they are especially useful for displaying and comparing relative differences in data with wide-ranging absolute values.

Bars are highly adaptable. They can be arranged either horizontally or vertically based on the overall layout of a visualization, space constraints, and labeling requirements. When combined with other media, such as points and lines, they make it easier to see and understand crucial contextual information—to consider the "compared to what?" and "so what?" questions essential to all successful data analysis and visualizations.

Bars are easy to create and easy to understand. They offer versatility in the design of beautiful, powerful displays of health and healthcare data. We know for sure that bars are *not* boring; only the unimaginative use of them is.

Bar Basics

Scale

Bar graphs must start at zero. When they display quantitative data, the entire length of the bar, including its endpoint, must be visible. Moreover, because the full length of the bar is its value, the starting point—its base—must be zero. If the bar begins at some other value, any real differences between all the bars displayed are distorted. Small differences look like large ones, which misleads viewers about actual values and any differences between them (Figure 6.3).

Resolutely ignore all assertions that the base of a bar graph does not have to start at zero—it does. There are times when a bar chart does not seem to be working for showing differences in data. Keep reading and you will learn ways that this versatile shape can be successfully adapted to manage these often-frustrating challenges!

Mock Data | Visual: HDV

FIGURE 6.3   Bar graphs must start at zero.

Bar Width and Spacing

If the width of the bars does not encode any additional information, they should all be the same width. The spaces between the bars should be the same width as the bar as well, that is, in a 1:1 ratio.

Bar Orientation

Is there a rule about a bar chart's orientation? No, but there are a few hints to govern the choice of vertical versus horizontal orientation.

Orienting for Labels and Space

Horizontal. If the categories of data displayed have long labels that would be hard to fit on the X-axis, and the audience is unfamiliar with them, orient the bars horizontally. Orienting the bars in this way also has the advantage of showing direct, descriptive, detailed labels (Figure 6.4, left).

Vertical. If the potential audience is familiar with the data and its abbreviations and acronyms, and there is limited horizontal space, it may be effective to arrange bars vertically and use shortened labels (Figure 6.4, right).

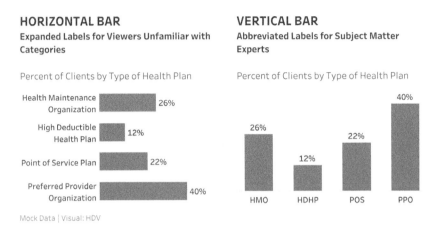

HORIZONTAL BAR
Expanded Labels for Viewers Unfamiliar with Categories

Percent of Clients by Type of Health Plan

VERTICAL BAR
Abbreviated Labels for Subject Matter Experts

Percent of Clients by Type of Health Plan

Mock Data | Visual: HDV

FIGURE 6.4   Bars may be oriented horizontally or vertically.

Trying both orientations takes very little time. Sketch or generate both versions to see which one works best, both for the intended audience and within any space constraints present.

Using Bars To: See How You're Doing

Distributions

Bars are the go-to graph type to show how frequently something is observed/occurs in a dataset. They may be oriented horizontally or vertically, and the base of the bar must always start at zero on the X- or Y-axis scale.

Histograms

A type of bar chart called a histogram (Figure 6.5) is most commonly used to show the frequency distribution of data, organized into "bins" of consecutive, non-overlapping intervals of a variable. The bins must be adjacent and of equal size. A distinguishing feature of histograms is that unlike other bar charts, they contain no, or minimal, spaces between bars, a design element that helps signal to the viewer that the variable on the X-axis is interval data.

Histograms are very useful for displaying the distribution of continuous intervals of data (such as ages, days, time) and determining if the data is distributed relatively evenly, is skewed, or is some other interesting shape, as in the examples in Figure 6.5.

HISTOGRAMS

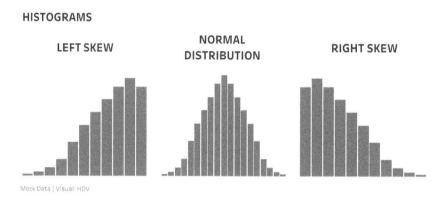

Mock Data | Visual: HDV

FIGURE 6.5   Histograms show frequency distributions of data.

Histograms are an excellent choice for displaying and communicating data distribution quickly and easily—as long as the "My Bin or Yours?" trap and the "Different Bin Size" conundrum can be avoided or managed. To explain:

In the example in Figure 6.6, the histogram on the left displays the percentage of low-risk Cesarean deliveries (C-sections) by maternal age in the United States (2017). The X-axis has divided maternal ages into bins, and a close look reveals the "My Bin or Yours?" trap. If a woman is 30 years old when she has a C-section, does she belong in the second bin (25–30 years) or the third (30–35)? On the histogram on the right, revised bin labels eliminate this overlap: now it is clear which bin each woman belongs in.

Another frequent challenge in health and healthcare analysis is that the data available are captured and reported in bins of unequal sizes—the "Different Bin Size" conundrum. One example is categories grouped on either side of the age spectrum: "0–18" or "80+" years, which requires the display of a bin size different from all other intervals, which are equal (20–29, 30–39, 40–49). To remedy this difficulty, leverage preattentive processing attributes (described in Chapter 4) to make the bar for the uniquely sized bin a different color from the others, thereby signaling "Look here: this bin is different."

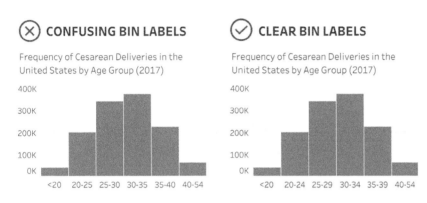

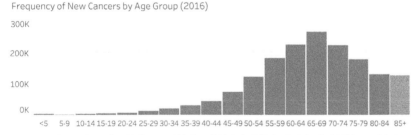

Data Sources: Martin JA, Hamilton BE, Osterman MJK, Driscoll AK, Drake P. Births: Final data for 2017. National Vital Statistics Reports; vol 67 no 8. Hyattsville, MD: National Center for Health Statistics and U.S. Department of Health and Human Services, Centers for Disease Control and Prevention and National Cancer Institute | Visual: HDV

FIGURE 6.6 Careful attention must be paid to histogram bin labels and sizes.

Population Pyramid (Paired Bars)

Another type of bar chart frequently found in the health and healthcare literature is called the population pyramid (Figure 6.7). Population pyramids are designed to show the age and sex composition/distribution, or other demographic information, of a specific population. They are often used by healthcare planners, researchers, and other health professionals to understand demographic transitions.

The arrangement of data on this type of chart is like that of a histogram but with a vertical orientation and paired bars extending out on either side of the axis, creating a shape that references a pyramid (hence the name).

The size of the population is displayed on the horizontal axis, and age is on the vertical axis. As is true for a histogram, the intervals of data must be equal and arranged sequentially, with the youngest age at the bottom and the oldest at the top.

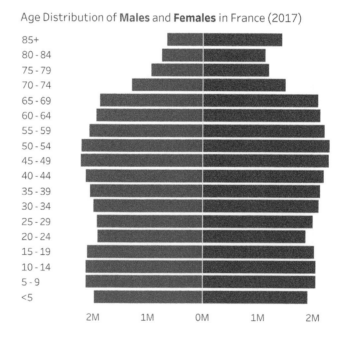

POPULATION PYRAMID (PAIRED BAR CHART)

Age Distribution of **Males** and **Females** in France (2017)

Data source: EuroStat Population by Broad Age Group and Sex | Visual: HDV

FIGURE 6.7 Population pyramids are also sometimes called paired bar charts.

Ranking

Displaying values in bar graphs in rank order affords a simple, elegant way to convey relative differences in health and health-care data (Figure 6.8). For example, "more versus fewer people (per 1,000 population) diagnosed with HIV in different countries," "hospitals that had the highest versus the lowest rate of hospital-acquired infections," or "those communities with the lowest vaccination rates." The decision to rank data values from high to low or low to high should be driven by the message that is most important for the intended viewers of data displays to consider. For example, low rates of HIV are usually desirable and high rates are not, so it often makes sense to call attention to the highest rates of HIV first.

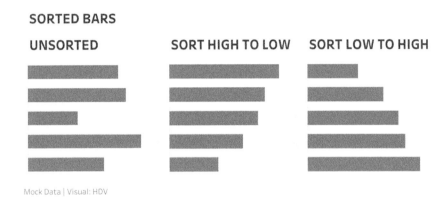

SORTED BARS

UNSORTED   **SORT HIGH TO LOW**   **SORT LOW TO HIGH**

Mock Data | Visual: HDV

FIGURE 6.8 Bar charts may be used to display unsorted or some sorted or rank order data.

Conversely, low vaccination rates are generally undesirable and high rates desirable. However, if the results of a new campaign against HIV, or a new push to raise vaccination rates, are being shown, the resulting lowered or raised rates may be the most important takeaway, and those should appear first in each case. The objective is always to create data visualizations that will make the central, most urgent message or the story in the data easy to see, understand, and, when appropriate, actionable.

Additional considerations about when and how to rank data (or when and how not to) may be determined by the way it is categorized (Chapter 2 covers several of these categories). In addition to organizing data structure, such categories make it clear why some data should *not* be arranged and displayed in rank order. For example:

- Ordinal data have some underlying natural order—for example, a pain scale from 1 to 10, or cancer stages I, II, III, IV. Therefore, displaying ordinal data out of its natural order, such as by ranking, may lead to misinterpretation because it is not in the expected sequence or arrangement. Ordinal data should not, therefore, be shown in rank order.

- Interval data are measured along a continuous scale, in which each point is placed at equal distance from every other point: age, time, or day ranges. As is true with ordinal data ranking, ranking interval data would render it illogical and difficult to understand. Therefore, interval data should not be ranked.

Change over Time

Time series data may be displayed using bars if it is essential to see the values in direct comparison to one another. The standard display used in these circumstances employs vertical bars with time increments ordered from oldest to most recent dates, like a line graph showing a trend over time. Arranging the data this way makes intuitive sense, as time is typically thought to move from the oldest to the most recent point, and from left to right along a continuum. Because seasonality is a frequent factor in health and healthcare data, displaying it over time using a bar graph may also be preferable for some results, as it helps present not only change but the distribution of results. In the example in Figure 6.9, the number of flu cases peaks during the winter. Evaluated with what a viewer probably knows from experience and training, this display makes complete sense.

Sometimes space constraints, or multiple periods to be displayed, make a horizontal bar chart the best choice. A decision is also needed as to data arrangement: Begin with the most recent results or the oldest ones?

BARS FOR DATE TRENDS

VERTICAL

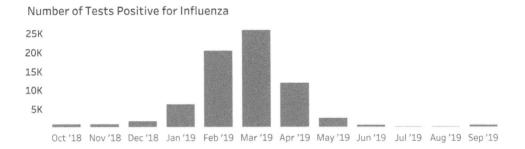

HORIZONTAL

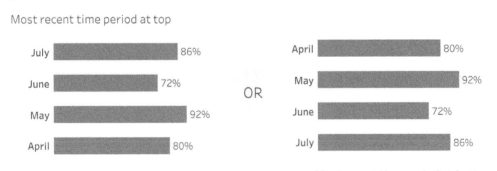

Mock Data | Visual: HDV

FIGURE 6.9   Bars may sometimes be used to display time series data.

As with all such presentations, the final determination should emerge in consultation and collaboration with a selection of end viewers to understand how they think about the sequencing of the results, and which time frame is most important to them.

Comparing Multiple Data Points

A bar chart like the one in Figure 6.10 may be used to see and compare multiple data points in several categories; however, it presents several challenges. First, it requires a key that has to be held in viewers' short-term memory and then matched to the bars. Second, because the bars displaying the same data points are not arranged near each other, it is difficult to make direct comparisons between them.

 SIDE-BY-SIDE BAR CHART

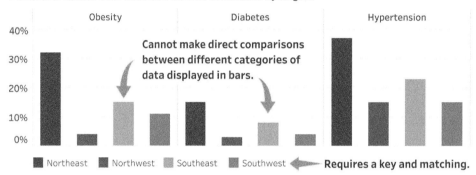

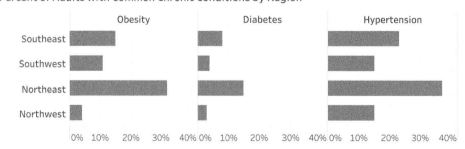

Mock Data | Visual: HDV

FIGURE 6.10 Small multiples are often a good choice to display different categories of data.

A much better technique for displaying these data is the use of a *small-multiples bar chart* (Tufte, 1990, 67). Small multiples are the go-to technique for displaying multiple data points that share some common categorization, such as geographic location, clinical services, or public health survey topics. This technique eliminates the need for a key and allows the viewer to directly compare each column and row of data.

As with many of the other bar charts described here and elsewhere, the decision about orienting data in a small-multiples chart horizontally or vertically depends on factors such as the most logical fit, the message to be displayed, and the overall arrangement of a dashboard, report, or infographic. Remember, it only takes a couple of minutes to sketch out a possible approach to help clarify and select the best arrangement.

Proportions | Part-to-Whole

Displaying parts-to-whole data can be challenging, and grasping the best techniques to display this type of data is not intuitive. Instead, it requires effort and study. Software applications may offer solutions that lead untrained users to believe they have only one option. An all-too-frequent result is an indecipherable chart, such as the "far-too-many-parts" stacked bar chart.

Stacked bar charts should be limited to two parts (or on rare occasions, three; see Figure 6.11). More than two parts render the additional values being displayed virtually impossible to interpret because any subsequent parts of the stacked bar begin and end at different places on the scale. An attempt to remedy this problem by layering an excess of labels onto different parts of the stacked bar simply does not work. Instead, it results only in a table of different-sized cells in a bewildering array of colors that is hard to view and understand.

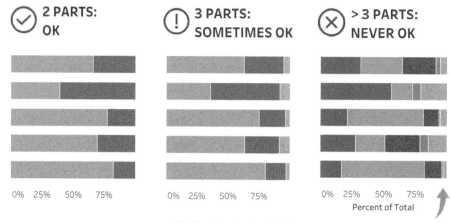

Mock Data | Visual: HDV

FIGURE 6.11   Stacked bar charts with more than three parts should be avoided.

A much better technique for displaying three or more parts of the whole is the use of a small-multiples bar chart (Figure 6.12). Creating a series of bar charts, all with the same axes and scale to show and compare different parts of the whole, makes it far easier to see and compare those parts. For example, in the following display,

SMALL MULTIPLES
To Show and Compare Parts of a Whole

Percent of Patients by Type of Care and Payor

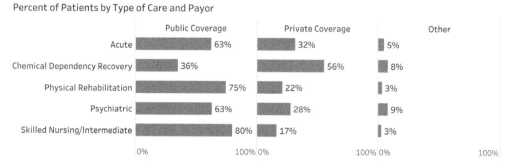

Mock Data | Visual: HDV

FIGURE 6.12   Small multiples provide a great solution for displaying parts-to-whole data.

reading across the different rows displaying the types of care makes clear the proportion (part) that each contributes. An added value is being able to compare directly the category of data displayed in each column. The ability to make these types of clear and direct comparisons is not possible by using a stacked bar chart with more than two (or on rare occasions, three) parts.

Challenging the 100% Myth

People often explain that they use a single chart like the "far-too-many-parts" stacked bar, or a pie or doughnut chart, to display parts-to-whole data because such charts definitively show that the different parts total 100%. However, this is a dangerous line of reasoning: if the underlying data do not add up to 100%, it is still possible to create these types of charts. (A quick web search for "funny charts that do not add up to 100%" will return a wealth of amusing examples.)

Additionally, confirming that the data add up to 100% is not what most viewers seek. Rather, what they seek and need to know is how the data are distributed, how the different parts (values) compare to each other or to a benchmark, whether the data are skewed, and/or the rank order of the data. None of these answers can be found easily through the use of stacked bars of more than two parts, or pie and donut charts.

It is easy to add wording to titles and headings to reassure viewers that the data totals to 100% or to add a label at the end of each bar showing its unique value so that the viewer can quickly make that calculation. Do not sacrifice display clarity to the 100% Myth.

Deviation (Difference, Variation)

A bar chart may also be used to display a deviation, that is, how one or more sets of quantitative values differ from a reference set of values. Bar charts are especially helpful in comparing relative differences or changes between groups that have a wide range of absolute values, such as departmental budgets versus actual results, or different countries' spending on healthcare services from one year versus that of another. By using a deviation bar graph to display the relative differences, the viewer can quickly identify which values are up or down, larger or smaller, and which ones could require further inquiry and analysis (Figure 6.13, top).

When the values displayed in a bar chart are very close to each other, and to a comparison value, like a target or goal, it can be hard to perceive the differences between the ends of the bars. Resist the temptation to break the best practice rule that bar charts start at zero! Instead, try displaying the data using a deviation bar chart that shows the difference from the comparison value (target or goal) of interest. Displaying data in this way allows the viewer to see both the value of the actual results (the end point of the scale of each bar) and the difference above or below the actual target (Figure 6.13, middle and bottom).

Ranges and Comparative Values

A floating bar chart may be used to display the range of a category of data, such as its minimum and maximum values, or beginning and ending values like start and stop times. It could also be used to display comparative data values, such as percentile results. Or they may be used to show confidence intervals of point estimates such as mortality observed vesus expected (O/E) ratios. Because the bars do not connect to a prescribed place on the axis, they have the appearance of floating—hence the name. Some examples of how floating bars have been used to display ranges of data include operational metrics such as hospital surgical case start and stop times and patient visit times in a clinic. They have also been used to communicate comparison percentile ranges for performance metrics such as patient experience surveys. In the following example, the addition of a point to encode the mean, median, or actual result on a given measure adds useful additional information (Figure 6.14, top).

Another type, a bullet graph (Few, 2006, 199), also uses a combination of bars (as well as line and color) to encode performance and comparison data. In the example in Figure 6.14 (bottom), the teal bar represents a group's performance on the metric of interest compared to the target they have set for themselves (black line); in the background,

DEVIATION BAR

To Show Relative Difference
Percent Difference Over/Under Budget by Department

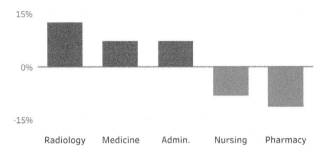

To Show Difference from a Goal or Target
Deviation of Patient Experience Score from Target by Department

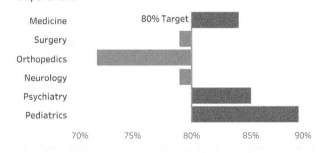

To Show Difference from a Goal or Target Over Time
Deviation of Patient Experience Score from Target by Quarter

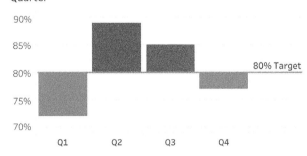

All charts are centered at the reference line.

Mock Data | Visual: HDV

FIGURE 6.13 Deviation charts make it easy to see differences and variations.

a bar of different gradients of the color gray displays comparative values such as national percentile results for the measures.

It is important to note that for these types of charts a key explaining the different elements being displayed should be placed directly near the display.

FLOATING BARS
To Display Value Range or a Range of Comparative Results

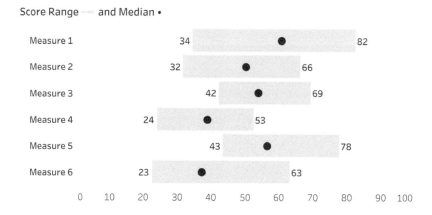

BULLET GRAPH
To Display Performance Compared to a Goal or Target

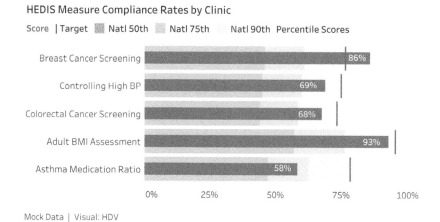

Mock Data | Visual: HDV

FIGURE 6.14 Floating bars and bullet graphs help to display ranges and comparative data.

To display a wide range of values (say, 500 to 10,000), two bar graphs with different axis ranges next to each other are useful (Figure 6.15). One bar graph shows only the lower values with the longer bars truncated while the other shows the full range of values. This simple technique allows a display of both the smallest and the largest values and makes clear the values' very wide range. This technique also follows the best practice of starting both bar graphs at zero.

LOW AND HIGH SIDE-BY-SIDE DISPLAY
When Showing a Wide Range of Values

Top 10 Countries in the Americas for Health Expenditures per Capita (in US$)

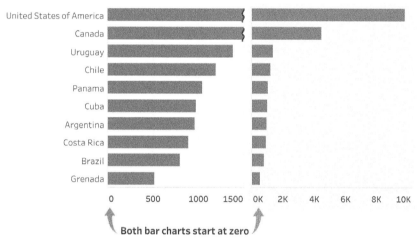

Data Source: Wolrd Health Organization Global Health Expenditure Database | Visual: HDV

FIGURE 6.15   Side-by-side bar charts may be created to show wide ranges of data values.

Displaying the Vital Few: Pareto Charts

In 1906, Italian social scientist and economist Vilfredo Pareto noted that 20% of the population of Italy owned 80% of the property. He put forward that this ratio could be found in many places in the physical world and hypothesized the presence of a natural law, where 80% of outcomes are determined by 20% of inputs.

Today this ratio is known as the "80/20 rule" or the "Pareto Principle." Its value is in reminding us to stay focused on the 20% (the "vital few") that matters—because those tasks or problems or factors will very likely produce 80% of results.

The Pareto chart, named in Pareto's honor, is specifically designed to display information so that the vital few stand out from the useful many. Its bars and lines illustrate which variables have the greatest cumulative effect on a given system, as in Figure 6.16.

PARETO CHART

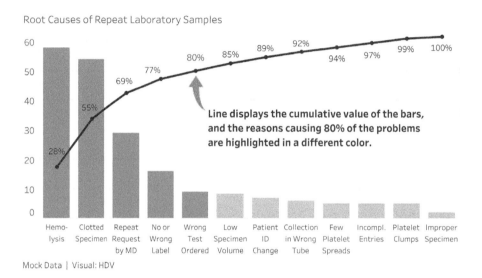

Root Causes of Repeat Laboratory Samples

Line displays the cumulative value of the bars, and the reasons causing 80% of the problems are highlighted in a different color.

Mock Data | Visual: HDV

FIGURE 6.16   Pareto charts show the 80/20 rule, or the "vital few."

Bars Are Not Boring

Bars truly are the workhorses of data visualization. Moreover, a solid understanding of how they are used will increase your confidence and skill as you create a range of simple-to-complex displays. We are also confident that as they become familiar and valuable tools, bars will reveal themselves as anything but boring. On the contrary: used correctly and imaginatively, they are beautiful in their ability to help viewers see and understand the critical stories in health and healthcare data.

Shape Two: Lines

Line charts are most often associated with displaying changes and trends in time series data. However, they can also help viewers see and consider frequency distributions, potential relationships or correlations between variables in the data, and as a reference/comparison value when combined with another chart shape.

Line Basics

Axis Scale and Aspect Ratios

Unlike bar charts, line graphs do not need to start at zero (Figure 6.17 top and bottom right). Bars encode data by their length; truncating the axis risks making small differences in health and healthcare data look like large ones, which can mislead viewers about the true values being displayed. Conversely, line graphs encode data by position or slope, so the zero baseline is less critical. What is essential, however, is the scale and the aspect ratio (i.e., the ratio of the data region's height to its width) used to display data on a line graph (Figure 6.17). There are no hard-and-fast rules about what the aspect ratio should be, but in general line graphs should be moderately greater in length than they are in height to emphasize the horizontal space versus the vertical space. Most important is that the aspect ratio should not be manipulated in a way that exaggerates the rate of change. As Tufte explains, time-series displays should be "lumpy," not spiky or flat.

Common vs. Logarithmic Scale

Typically, a common linear scale where the size of the interval from one tick mark to the next is the same (e.g., 1, 2, 3, 4, 5) is used to display data. Logarithmic (log) scales are a different scale where each tick mark represents a tenfold increase over the previous one (e.g., 1, 10, 100, 1,000, 10,000). Although log scales based on a factor of ten are the easiest to understand, the interval on a log scale can be a factor of 2, or 5, or 27, or any other number.

Depending on the data and the message that needs to be conveyed, log scales are an option that should be considered.

LINE SCALES

Life expectancy at Birth in Years (1970-2017)   Overall | Male | Female

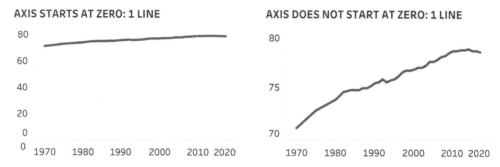

The y-axis on both charts ends at 80, but by beginning the one on the right at 70, we can more easily see the values of the line and variations over time.

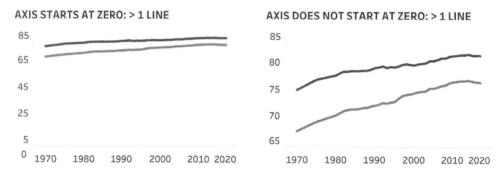

The y-axis on both charts ends at 85, but by beginning the one on the right at 65, we can more easily see the values of the line, variations over time and differences between groups.

Data Source: NCHS, National Vital Statistics System, public-use Mortality Files | Visual: HDV

FIGURE 6.17   Careful attention must be paid to line graph axis scale and aspect ratios.

For example, log scales can emphasize the rate of change in a way that linear scales do not and if that is the key message to be communicated, it may be a better choice than a common scale. Again, keep in mind they are less intuitive, and depending on the experience of the viewer with this type of scale, may be harder to understand than linear scales.

Limit Lines | Consider Small Multiples

Limit the number of lines on one display to no more than four (Figure 6.18, top). Line graphs with too many different categories of data in a single display become cluttered very quickly and are difficult to understand. As discussed in the bar section of this chapter (above), it is useful to create small multiples of line graphs when several groups or categories are to be compared on one graph (Figure 6.18, bottom).

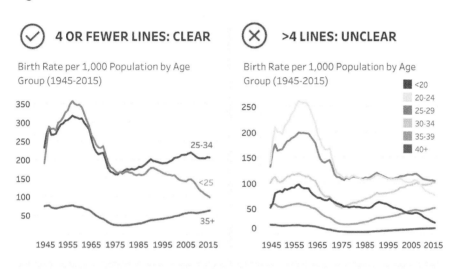

Data Sources: Hamilton BE, Lu L, Chong Y, et al. Natality trends in the United States, 1909-2015. National Center for Health Statistics. 2017. Designed by L Lu, BE Hamilton, L. Rossen, A Lipphardt, JM Keralis, and Y Chong: CDC/National Center for Health Statistics. | Visual: HDV

FIGURE 6.18   Limit lines to avoid clutter and loss of clarity (consider using small multiples).

Missing Data and Actual vs. Forecast Data

Missing data must be shown as a gap on a line graph displaying continuous data. Viewers tend to be highly suspicious of lines that display zero as a result, and that is a logical response. Zero is a real value; if it is in a dataset, it should be included and displayed on a line graph of continuous data. (If you have two cookies and I have zero, that is a very real and sad number for me.) However, missing data are sometimes mistakenly entered as a value of zero on a spreadsheet or in a data table and then incorrectly displayed as a zero result on a line graph, when in fact there are no results to report. It is crucial to display missing data by showing a gap or break in lines.

A continuous line displaying a combination of actual versus fore-casted data must be displayed using different types of lines, for example, a solid line for actual data, changing to a dash line for forecast data to ensure that viewers understand that two different values are being displayed.

The design techniques shown in Figure 6.19 are another example of leveraging preattentive attributes and signaling to the viewer that "there is something different in these data you need to be aware of."

LINE WITH MISSING DATA

Prevalence of New York City Residents who Participated in Exercise in the Past 30 days (2002-2017, age-adjusted estimate)

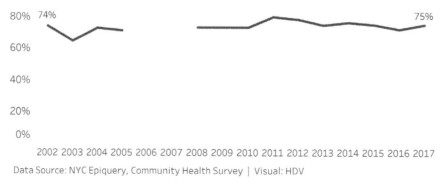

Data Source: NYC Epiquery, Community Health Survey | Visual: HDV

FIGURE 6.19 Leverage preattentive attributes to show missing or different data on a line.

LINE WITH FORECASTED DATA

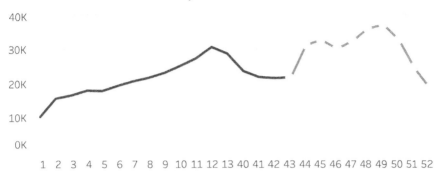

Actual and Forecasted Revenue by Week Number

Mock Data | Visual: HDV

FIGURE 6.19   (Continued)

Using Lines To: See How You're Doing

As a Reference | Comparison

Everything in data analysis and visualization is grounded in the core concept of "compared with what?" Using a line in combination with another encoding method, such as a point or bar as shown in Figure 6.20, offers a technique to answer this question.

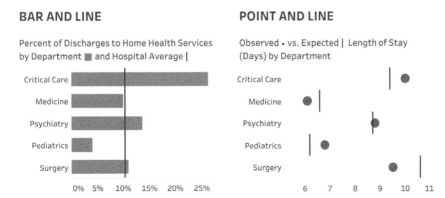

BAR AND LINE

Percent of Discharges to Home Health Services by Department ▆ and Hospital Average |

POINT AND LINE

Observed • vs. Expected | Length of Stay (Days) by Department

Reference line can be a summary measure for the entire chart or unique to each row or column.

Mock Data | Visual: HDV

FIGURE 6.20   Reference lines provide context to data.

Change over Time

Line graphs display trends or changes in data over time (Figure 6.21).

LINE GRAPH

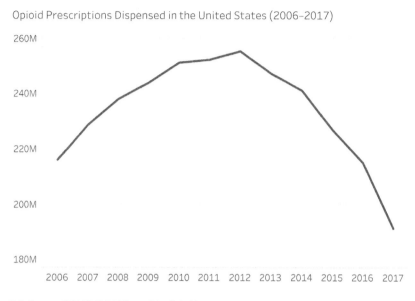

Opioid Prescriptions Dispensed in the United States (2006–2017)

Data Source: CDC U.S. Opioid Prescribing Rate Maps,
https://www.cdc.gov/drugoverdose/maps/rxrate-maps.html | Visual: HDV

FIGURE 6.21   Use a line graph to show change over time.

A line can also display two data periods with changes that have occurred between them (Year 1 versus Year 2). The simplicity of the line connecting the two points in time on a slopegraph makes it easy to see and compare values quickly (Figure 6.22, top). It also makes it easy to consider the magnitude of any change (as illustrated by the slope of the lines), any change in direction (upward/increasing, downward/decreasing), and any changes in values ranking. A bump chart is a type of slopegraph that can be used to show, at different intervals of time, how one value may be "bumped" by another, thereby changing its rank. When the first message to be conveyed is about how values rank and changes to rank at different points in time, a bump chart can be the right choice (Figure 6.22, bottom).

SLOPE GRAPH

Government Expenditures on Health as Percent of Total Government Expenditures (1995 and 2013)

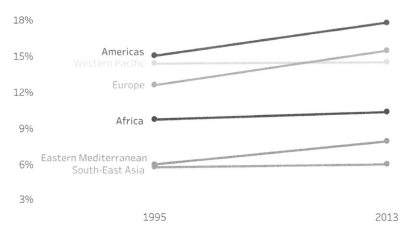

BUMP CHART

Change in Rank for Cancers with the Highest 5-Year Survival Rate (1977-2013)

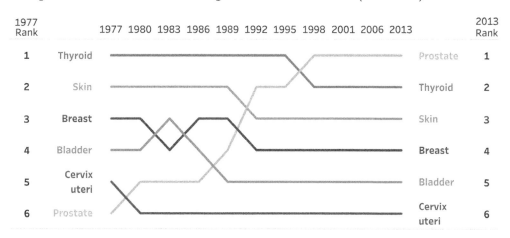

Data Sources: World Health Organization Global Health Observatory (slope graph); Our World in Data, Cancer death rates are falling; five-year survival rates are rising (bump chart) | Visual: HDV

FIGURE 6.22   Slopegraphs and bump charts show change over time and rank.

Change over Time | Sparklines

Edward Tufte coined the term *sparkline* in his book, *Beautiful Evidence*:

> These little data lines, because of their active quality over time, are named *sparklines*—small, high-resolution graphics usually embedded in a full context of words, numbers, images. Sparklines are *datawords*: data-intense, design-simple, word-sized graphics. (2006, 47)

Typically displayed without axes or coordinates, sparklines present trends and variations associated with some measurement of frequent "sparks" of data in a simple and condensed way. They can be small enough to insert into a line of text, or several sparklines may be grouped as elements of a small-multiple chart (Figure 6.23).

SPARKLINES

24-Hour Patient Vital Signs and Normal Range

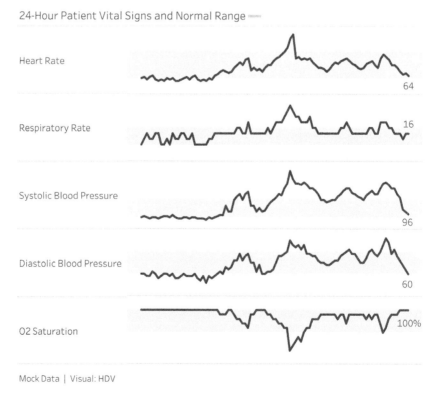

Mock Data | Visual: HDV

FIGURE 6.23 Sparklines display frequent sparks of data in a condensed way.

Change over Time | Deviation Graphs

Sometimes it is necessary to show only the relative change in a value over time—for example, whether an emergency department is treating more or fewer patients this year compared to last. It is often more useful to see relative change rather than absolute values. Alternatively, an organization may need to monitor (at a very high level) whether it is over or under budget on a rolling 12-month basis. Again, the absolute value is less important than the change as a dollar amount or percentage. In both cases, viewers need only answer the question, "Over time, are we up or down, and by how much?" Here, a deviation line graph is a simple, elegant way to display relative changes over time (Figure 6.24). The addition of color also helps viewers to quickly see when the values are above or below the reference line (leveraging human preattentive processing). It is also an example of the Gestalt Principle of Continuity, which states (in part) that the eye tends to want to follow a line from one end to the other, even when the line's color changes.

DEVIATION LINE

Monthly Emergency Department Patient Volume, Percent Change from Prior Year

Mock Data | Visual: HDV

DEVIATION LINE WITH COLOR

Monthly Expenses, Percent Difference from Budget Over budget | Under budget

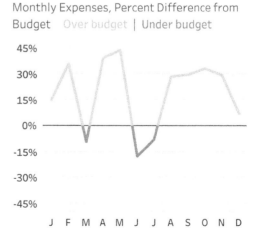

FIGURE 6.24 Deviation line graphs help viewers to quickly see relative changes over time.

Distributions

Like the bars on histograms, lines may be used for understanding the shapes of distributions in a type of graph called a frequency polygon. A cumulative frequency polygon is the same as a frequency distribution graph, except that the Y-axis value for each point is the number in the corresponding class interval plus all numbers in the lower intervals (Figure 6.25). Two lines may also be used on both of these types of frequency polygons to compare two distributions.

FREQUENCY POLYGON

New Salmonella Cases by Date of Illness Onset

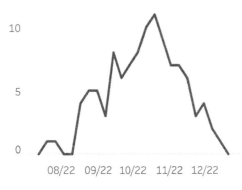

CUMULATIVE FREQUENCY POLYGON

Cumulative Salmonella Cases by Date

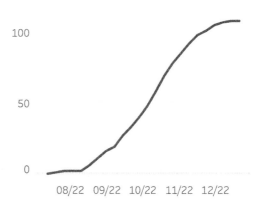

Mock data | Visual: HDV

FIGURE 6.25   Frequency polygons show the shape of distributions.

Distributions | The Empirical Rule and Control Charts

This is not a book about statistics. However, as more analysis is undertaken and widely disseminated by health and healthcare organizations, especially about the quality of care being delivered, it seems important to include a brief overview of the empirical rule and control charts.

When the values being displayed have a normal distribution, adding lines to show one, two, and three standard deviations from the mean can help the viewer to gain additional insights through something called the empirical rule (also called the three-sigma or the 68, 95, 99.7 rule as shown in Figure 6.26). In statistics this rule states that when values have a normal distribution, almost all of the data will fall within three standard deviations of the mean. Therefore, when the data being displayed have a normal distribution (which results in a bell-shaped curve) additional annotations may be made about the spread of the data to help the viewer understand that:

- 68% of data are within 1 standard deviation.
- 95% of data are within 2 standard deviations.
- 99.7% of data are within 3 standard deviations.

EMPIRICAL RULE

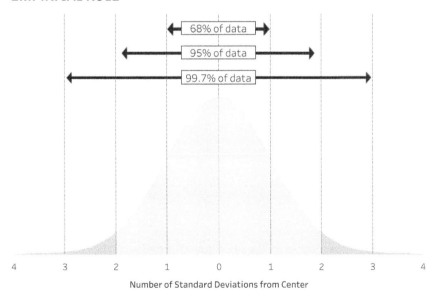

FIGURE 6.26 The empirical rule provides additional insights.

Statistical Process Control Charts (SPCs) and Geometric (G) Charts

Statistical process control (SPC) is a method of quality control which employs statistical methods to monitor and control a process. SPCs are used to distinguish between common cause and special cause variances in a process.

Data are usually displayed over time and in time order but can also be for just a particular point in time. The chart will include a center-line (usually the statistical mean), data points, and statistically calculated upper and lower three-sigma limits (i.e., the variation from the mean as described in the empirical rule above) also displayed with lines (Figure 6.27).

CONTROL CHART

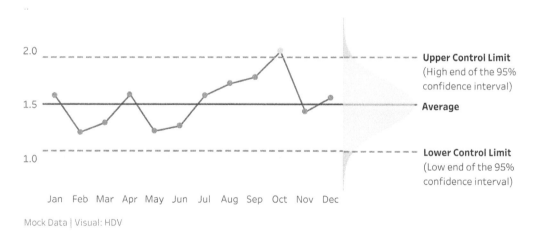

Mock Data | Visual: HDV

FIGURE 6.27 Distinguishing between common cause vs. special cause variances.

The use of control charts by healthcare providers to capture information about the quality of care being delivered has increased dramatically. It is important to understand, however, that one size control chart does not fit all. For example, a G chart, based on the geometric distribution, is designed specifically for monitoring rare events. They typically plot the number of days between rare events or the number of opportunities (e.g., count of surgeries) between rare events. Other outcomes, such as mortality, are best communicated as observed versus expected ratios with accompanying confidence intervals, and not on control charts. Bottom line, control charts are not one-size-fits-all and must be used carefully and appropriately with audiences who understand how to interpret them.

Relationships | Correlations

Chapter 4 describes the Gestalt (Pattern) Principle of Proximity and how the human eye perceives connections between visual elements. This specific principle explains the need to include a line on a scatterplot (Figure 6.28). This element, called a trendline, helps determine if there is any correlation (connection or relationship, not causation)

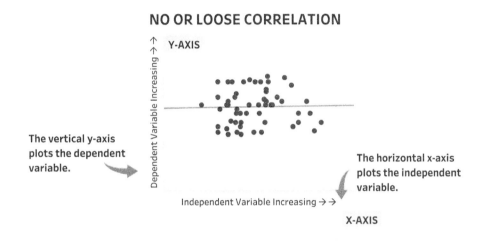

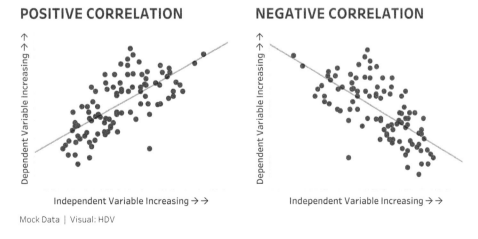

Mock Data | Visual: HDV

FIGURE 6.28 Lines on scatterplots help viewers to see potential connections between variables.

between the variables being displayed. The distance or proximity of variables being plotted from the line signal whether there is a close, loose, or nonexistent correlation between variables. The closer the points cluster to the line, the stronger the correlation; the further away, the looser it is. The direction of the line helps show how the variables may be correlated: Are they moving up/increasing together (positively correlated) or moving down/decreasing together (negatively correlated)? Or is the correlation loose or nonexistent?

This simple example reinforces the importance of research on vision and cognition: it is essential to understanding why and how specific techniques help to make displays of data both clear and compelling.

Shape Three: Points

Points help viewers to see and compare unique values in health and healthcare data. Points can stand alone or may be used in combination with other graph types (some already discussed, others discussed below). They add important details and create a revelatory context that permits fuller consideration and understanding of the data displayed.

Point Basics

Axes Scale

Using points (instead of a bar chart) to display values affords the option of not having to start the scale at zero (see Figure 6.30). As we explained in the previous section, when bar charts start at some value other than zero, any real differences between them can be distorted. This distortion is not a problem when points are used, and therefore the scale can start at some value other than zero.

Differentiating Points

When points are used to encode a single variable, it is easy for viewers to identify what they are seeing. Note, however, that when points encode two or more variables, they must be differentiated in some way (Figure 6.29). To achieve this, refer again to the Gestalt

SHAPE POINTS

SINGLE SHAPE POINT

Sugary Drink Consumption

◀ Lower is better

13%

◀

State: 23%

In County 1, the percent of adults 18 years and older who report drinking one or more 12 ounce sugar-sweetened beverage (sodas, fruit punch, sweet iced tea, sports drinks, etc.) on average per day is 13%. It is good when this goes down and it is currently lower than the state as a whole.

MULTIPLE SHAPE POINTS

Correlation of BMI and Systolic Blood Pressure among Patients with a BMI above + and below ○ 30

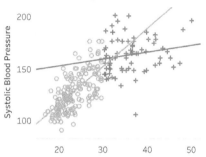

FILLED   **UNFILLED**   **TRANSPARENT**

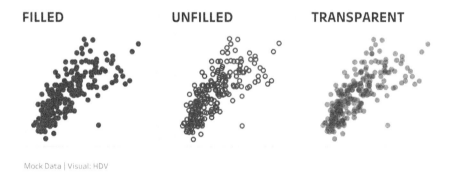

Mock Data | Visual: HDV

FIGURE 6.29   Techniques to differentiate points.

Principle of Similarity discussed in Chapter 4 (things that share visual characteristics, such as color, shape, or size, will be seen as belonging together).

Color (sometimes called *hue*; see note below). Color is often the best method of visually differentiating between points. However, if the variables overlap, some of them may be obscured by others.

In order to prevent this problem, some fill can be removed from the points, creating enough transparency to allow viewers to see those that overlap.

(Note: The terms *color* and *hue* are often used interchangeably as if they meant the same thing, even though—in the technical terms of color analysis—they do not. For the sake of simplicity, the term *color* has been used here throughout.)

Shape (referred to as "shape points"). We can use alternatives to a point such as a box, circle, triangle, cross, or X to display multivariate data.

Using Points To: See How You're Doing
Distributions

Although bars are the go-to graph to show the number, frequency, distribution, or other measures (such as a statistical mean or median) for different discrete categories of data, using a point instead of a bar has its advantages. With limited space or displayed values across a wide range, the ability to start a scale at a value other than zero can be advantageous (Figure 6.30).

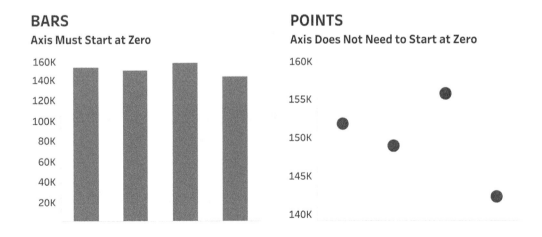

Mock Data | Visual: HDV

FIGURE 6.30   Points may sometimes be used to show distributions.

Revealing Details

A type of display called a *dot strip plot* effectively presents additional details about the range (the difference between the highest and lowest values) displayed. (A dot is a pronounced point.) The bar section, above, showed how a floating bar is used to display a summary view of the range (Figure 6.14). Using a dot strip plot to display the same underlying data provides the added advantage of highlighting where the data may cluster and identifying outliers (Figure 6.31, top). Applying a technique called "jittering" makes the dots on a strip plot more clearly visible by separating them, so they are not plotted directly on top of one other (Figure 6.31, bottom).

STRIP PLOT

Age Distribution of Cardiovascular Clinic Patients by Race Compared to Median (line)

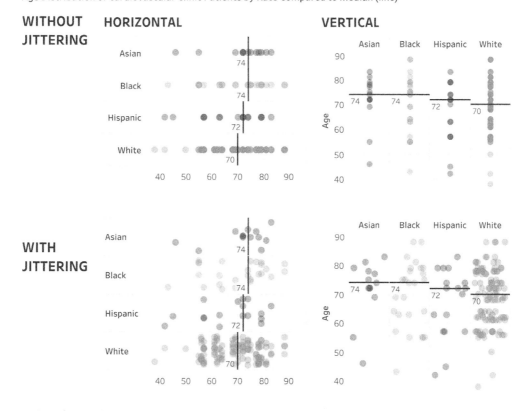

Mock Data | Visual: HDV

FIGURE 6.31   Dot strip plots provide details about a range of data.

Change over Time

Line graphs in themselves make it easy to see how values have changed over time, and do not require the addition of points. However, if there are multiple lines on a chart, and a need to compare their specific values, the addition of points can help viewers pinpoint (pun intended) values more easily (Figure 6.32).

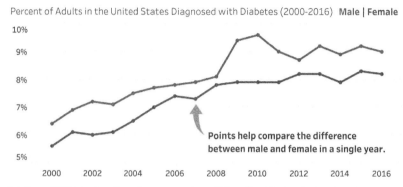

LINE WITH POINTS
To Help Compare the Difference Between Two Values

Percent of Adults in the United States Diagnosed with Diabetes (2000-2016) **Male | Female**

Points help compare the difference between male and female in a single year.

Data Source: US Diabetes Surveillance System; www.cdc.gov/diabetes/data; Division of Diabetes Translation - Centers for Disease Control and Prevention | Visual: HDV

FIGURE 6.32   The addition of points on lines helps viewers make comparisons.

Correlation

As shown in the previous section about lines, the scatter plot is a two-dimensional data visualization that uses points to represent the values obtained for two different variables (Figure 6.28). When creating a scatter plot to determine if there is a potential correlation between variables, the independent variable is placed on the X-axis and the dependent variable on the Y-axis. In any dataset, the independent or X-variable is the one chosen or manipulated by the researcher/experimenter. The dependent or Y-variable is the one whose value depends on or is affected by the value of the independent variable. (Reminder: Use care in labeling the scatter chart: correlation is not causation.)

Hierarchy Quadrant

A simple quadrant can be a very effective way to display a hierarchy of the combination of data values such as the risk-score of patients being treated and the cost of that care by different provider groups. The Y-axis in Figure 6.33 is the patient risk-score and the X-axis is the Per Member Per Month (PMPM) cost. Points are used to plot each unique provider group's results. Lines are used to show all groups' scores for both values and serve to create quadrants that are labeled by the hierarchies of results: Low Cost/High Risk; High Cost/High Risk; Low Cost/Low Risk; High Cost/Low Risk. In this example, displaying the data in these quadrants and labeled in this manner is a quick and easy way to identify the best-performing (Low Cost/High Risk) and the groups that may need to improve the most (High Cost/Low Risk).

PERFORMANCE QUADRANT

Patient Risk and Per Member Per Month (PMPM) Cost by Provider Group

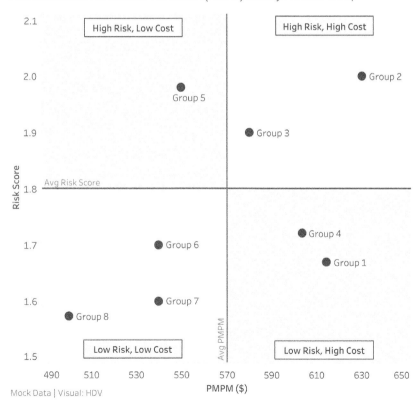

Mock Data | Visual: HDV

FIGURE 6.33   A quadrant is a simple way to show a hierarchy of two variables.

Location Details

Points may be overlaid on maps to mark the specific location of, for example, healthcare facilities in relation to populations with specific diagnoses or the incidence or prevalence of diseases and conditions. In Figure 6.34, points have been used to illustrate the number and location of Certified Healthcare Facilities in Southern California as compared to the population in each ZIP code (see Chapter 7 for more about choropleth maps).

POINTS OVERLAID ON CHOROPLETH MAP

Location of Health Facilities in Southern California Compared to Population Den..

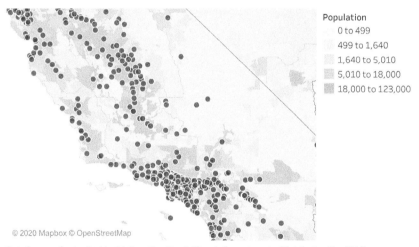

Data Source: Center for Health Care Quality, California Department of Public Health. 2018. HealthcareFacilities-California_2018-09-05-CA-CDPH and 2016 Community Health Survey | Visual: HDV

FIGURE 6.34   Points on a map provide additional details.

Shape Four: Boxes

It has been widely and accurately argued that what are sometimes referred to as boxes in data visualizations are actually bars. For example, Princeton statistician John Tukey, a data visualization creator and leading expert in the field, used the term *box* instead of *bar* when he named his invention to display quartiles of data the "box-and-whisker" plot. (It should be added that someone who creates a chart as brilliant as the box-and-whisker can call it anything he wants.) It is also true that in some cases, there is no question that a box is the shape being used to display data. Ben Shneiderman, at the University of Maryland, used boxes (and rectangles) to display complex hierarchical data in a type of chart he named a *treemap*. Software designer Cormac Kinney coined the term *heatmap* to describe a display of values represented by boxes of different saturations of color to represent high and low values in a manner similar to choropleth maps (see Chapter 7 for more information about maps).

Box Basics

Color Selection

The use of a palette visible to the colorblind is crucial to ensure that all viewers can see variations in data displayed. All too often, heatmaps and treemaps use red and green to encode "good" or "bad" performance or change, rendering them unusable by people who are red/green colorblind (learn more about this phenomenon in Chapter 9).

Correct Use

Boxes are often used to create advanced/complex data visualizations such as a box-and-whisker plot or a treemap, designed to solve particular data visualization challenges. Understanding their features as well as the problems they were invented to solve is essential to using them correctly.

Using Boxes To: See How You're Doing

Distribution

Boxes combined with lines make it possible to depict groups of numerical data through their quartiles. The box-and-whisker plot created by John Tukey illustrates the clarity and efficiency of this data-visualization technique. Points overlaid on a box-and-whisker plot also display data in each quartile precisely, enhancing the ability to see outliers that might be hidden in a more traditional display (Figure 6.35).

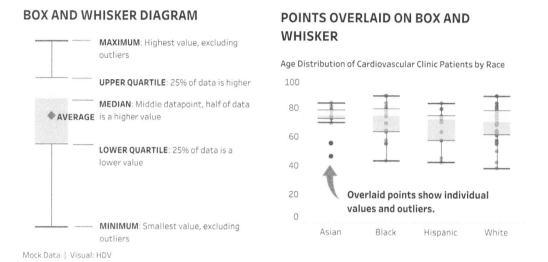

BOX AND WHISKER DIAGRAM

MAXIMUM: Highest value, excluding outliers

UPPER QUARTILE: 25% of data is higher

MEDIAN: Middle datapoint, half of data is a higher value

AVERAGE

LOWER QUARTILE: 25% of data is a lower value

MINIMUM: Smallest value, excluding outliers

Mock Data | Visual: HDV

POINTS OVERLAID ON BOX AND WHISKER

Age Distribution of Cardiovascular Clinic Patients by Race

Overlaid points show individual values and outliers.

Asian   Black   Hispanic   White

FIGURE 6.35   Box-and-whisker plots provider greater insights about the distribution of data.

(Note: Care must be taken to avoid applying this level of detail to any public or unsecured displays of patient data that would make it identifiable.)

Multiple Values

It is sometimes useful to quickly and easily display a large number of categories of data while highlighting the high and low values present. Using boxes to arrange data so it can be easily cross-referenced, and the categories compared, then adding varying color saturation to signal high and low values, is a great way to display a large amount of information economically (Figure 6.36).

HEATMAP

U.S. Healthcare Expenditures in Billions by Type and Payor (2017)

% of Total 2017 Expense

0% [gradient bar] 15%

	Medicaid	Medicare	Other Health Insurance Programs	Other Third Party Payers	Out of Pocket	Private Health Insurance
Hospital Care	$193.9	$282.9	$69.6	$106.9	$33.9	$455.3
Physician and Clinical Services	$75.3	$159.0	$32.3	$66.7	$60.1	$300.9
Prescription Drugs	$33.0	$100.9	$11.0	$1.8	$46.7	$140.1
Other Health Care	$105.9	$5.0	$2.5	$49.6	$6.5	$13.6
Nursing Care Facilities	$50.2	$37.7	$5.4	$12.1	$44.3	$16.6
Dental Services	$12.5	$0.9	$4.0	$0.5	$53.0	$58.2
Other Medical	$7.9	$10.1	$0.2	$0.9	$88.1	$11.4
Home Health	$35.0	$38.8	$0.7	$2.7	$9.0	$10.8
Other Professional Services	$7.5	$24.7	$0.4	$7.2	$23.9	$33.0

Data Source: CMS.gov | Visual: HDV

FIGURE 6.36   Heatmap tables are useful to display many categories of data.

Change over Time and Utilization Rates

A heatmap can also show how data have changed over time (Figure 6.37). This technique is especially useful on a dashboard where the data are large but space is small. Heatmaps also effectively display many precise data points, such as a calendar-type view of a clinic's use of available appointment time by the hours and days of the week.

Hierarchical Data

Boxes are the foundation of a treemap (created by Ben Shneiderman at the University of Maryland). Shneiderman designed this type of display to present hierarchical data (for example, all countries, unique countries, causes of death in each country, and a change

HEATMAP

Slot Utilization Rate by Day of the Week

Slot Utilization Rate

0% [   ] 40%

	Mon		Tues		Weds		Thurs		Fri		Sat	
	Slot Minutes Used	Slot Utilization Rate	Slot Minutes Used	Slot Utilization Rate	Slot Minutes Used	Slot Utilization Rate	Slot Minutes Used	Slot Utilization Rate	Slot Minutes Used	Slot Utilization Rate	Slot Minutes Used	Slot Utilization Rate
7:00	1,050	19%	2,135	27%	1,435	25%	1,285	25%	1,220	23%	775	31%
8:00	2,945	19%	4,885	23%	3,565	22%	4,420	24%	2,725	18%	815	34%
9:00	5,675	24%	6,105	22%	5,645	25%	6,210	24%	4,230	21%	795	34%
10:00	5,495	23%	7,190	25%	5,535	24%	6,170	24%	3,900	19%	620	28%
11:00	5,525	24%	5,975	22%	4,635	21%	5,100	21%	3,745	19%		
13:00	4,820	20%	5,090	20%	5,285	21%	3,110	15%	2,410	14%		
14:00	5,645	23%	5,370	22%	5,125	21%	3,770	18%	2,215	13%		
15:00	5,050	22%	4,920	21%	4,435	19%	3,880	19%	1,865	12%		
16:00	3,945	19%	3,210	16%	3,355	18%	2,650	14%	1,305	10%		
17:00	2,125	25%	1,560	21%	1,750	21%	1,380	20%	270	10%		
18:00	1,350	32%	800	26%	1,120	31%	380	13%	110	7%		
19:00	30	40%	30	40%	30	40%	380	13%	110	7%		

Mock Data | Visual: HDV

FIGURE 6.37 Heatmap tables can be useful to display time series data.

in the values from one period to another) that could not be easily displayed in a bar chart (Figure 6.38). Chapter 8 discusses the most frequent misuses of treemaps and offers suggestions for correcting these errors.

Other Shapes

Round shapes—pies, donuts, and bubbles—have not been forgotten, but they are in nearly all cases to be avoided. Chapter 8 discusses their significant limitations and why, based on human

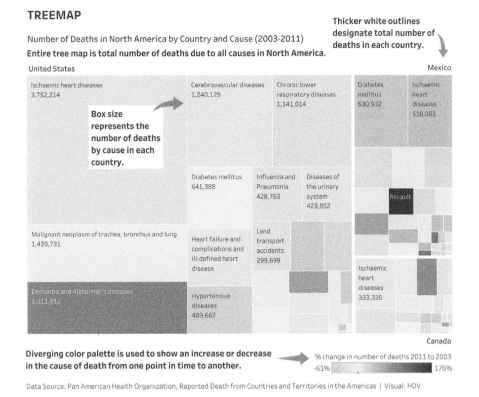

FIGURE 6.38   Treemaps are a special type of display designed to show hierarchal data.

cognition and the best practices of data visualization, they should never be used or at least used with great caution.

Summary

At the beginning of this chapter, we asserted that "it is incredible how many displays of data can be created using bars, lines, points, and boxes (alone and in combination) to create elegantly simple yet powerfully effective visualizations." Understanding the genesis, uses, and advantages of displays based on these four shapes will build your confidence and skill in designing compelling, revelatory views of health and healthcare data.

Chapter Seven

Maps

Using Maps to Gain Insights

Geographic Maps

Geographic maps are abstractions that allow features in the real world to be represented digitally or on paper. They rely on the arrangement of information, and on spatial relationships between elements of that information, to convey meaning.

Overlaying one or more data elements on a geographic map allows better presentation and a more precise understanding of the differences or similarities between geographic areas. These features and capacities make geographic data maps a powerful and intuitive way to show geospatial data.

Four useful types of maps can help visualize health and healthcare data: choropleth, hex-tile, symbol/dot-density, and proportional dot-density maps.

Choropleth Maps

A *choropleth* (from the Greek words for "area/region" and "multitude") is a thematic map in which areas are shaded or patterned in proportion to the measure being displayed. They are an easy way to visualize how a measurement varies across a geographic area, or to show the level of variability within a region. Color saturation corresponds to a measure's value, typically with more saturated color representing higher values and less saturated color representing lower values.

Choropleth maps were a complete game-changer two decades ago when they were used by Dr. Jack Wennberg, founder of the Dartmouth Atlas Project, to show glaring variations in medical resources distribution and use in the United States. Their impact has been profound, raising awareness of the disparities in healthcare delivery in the U.S. system and moving people to question the status quo.

Choropleth maps are very intuitive and easy to use for quick, at-a-glance insights. Consider the example in Figure 7.1, which shows the percent of people without health insurance by state.

CHOROPLETH MAP

Percent of People without Health Insurance by State (2018)

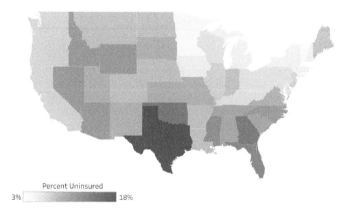

Percent Uninsured

3%   18%

Data Source: Kaiser Family Foundation, Health Insurance Coverage of the Total Population, 2018 | Visual: HDV

FIGURE 7.1 Choropleth map.

The user will easily recognize the shape of the United States, and without needing to reference the legend, will quickly intuit that darker means higher. It takes only a couple of seconds to see that Texas has the highest uninsured rate and Massachusetts the lowest. Labels could be added to indicate the ranking of every state or to select states of particular interest (such as the highest and lowest). This display's primary power is its ability to let the viewer quickly and easily see and understand where variation occurs across the country—to grasp and process high-level insights quickly. Each region is shown familiarly (closely), with its actual map shape showing size, borders, and relation to other states.

Choropleth maps can be displayed at any geographic level: by country, region, state, county, ZIP code, census tract, and many other characteristics.

However, there are parameters and limitations to keep in mind when using choropleth maps. To state the obvious first: each shaded area corresponds to the landmass of that geographic region, not the number of people who live there. This feature can give more implicit weight, or importance, to larger regions with fewer people.

For example, Wyoming has one of the highest uninsured rates, New York, one of the lower ones. However, New York—much more densely populated than Wyoming—has far more uninsured people.

Population density variations can often be accounted for by the use of normalized metrics such as rates or a measure per capita. For something like health insurance that is influenced by state-level policy, the normalized metric of rate by the state makes sense.

However, if a display's user needs to know where to target an intervention to reach the largest number of people, normalized metrics may not be the right choice. Take, for example, the maps in Figure 7.2, which show teen births in Colorado by county—rates on the left, counts on the right. If rates alone were considered in the

determination of where to target efforts, the more densely populated counties where most teen births occur might be overlooked.
As with any data visualization, it is essential to carefully consider the
intended use and purpose of maps when choosing the measure
to display.

Choropleth Maps: Choose Metrics Carefully

Birth Rate per 1,000 Females Age 15-19 Years by
County in Colorado (2018)

Number of Births among Females Age 15-19 Years
by County in Colorado (2018)

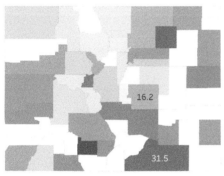

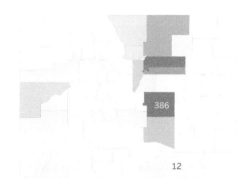

Data Source: Vital Statsitics Program, Colorado Department of Public Health and Environment | Visual: HDV

FIGURE 7.2   Choosing metrics carefully.

Despite the intuitive, grasp-and-go nature of choropleth maps, they
can, ironically, be overwhelming. The gradient (light to dark of a single color) color palette typically used for these maps results in slight
saturation or hue variations that can be hard to distinguish between,
especially in areas not neighboring one another. The advantage of
this characteristic is that the user easily sees geographic variation;
the downside is that it may be harder to see what regions to focus
on. To set off areas needing the viewer's attention (those with the
highest and/or lowest values, for example), consider using threshold shading where values below or above specific cutoff points are
highlighted in different colors.

CHOROPLETH MAP WITH THRESHOLD SHADING

States Where **More than 10% of People are without Health Insurance** (2018)

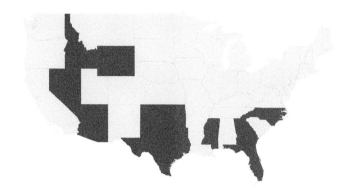

Data Source: Kaiser Family Foundation, Health Insurance Coverage of the Total Population, 2018 | Visual: HDV

FIGURE 7.3   Choropleth map with threshold shading.

Hex-Tile Maps

Hex-tile maps represent geographic areas with hexagons placed in proximity to their true location and color shaded in relation to the value of the measure being shown. In the hex map in Figure 7.4, viewers can recognize the more abstract shape of the United States, with each state having (more or less) its actual neighbors.

In the hex map, each state is the same size, eliminating any potential incorrect perception about the proportions of the information being displayed on a traditional geographic map. This feature also removes what is sometimes referred to as "the Alaska Effect": the distraction or misperception caused by Alaska being huge (twice the size of Texas) and far away from the lower 48. A hex map also allows the viewer to see the color and label of the smallest state as easily as the largest state. When a simple yes/no proposition, such as whether a particular healthcare program exists in a specific state, is being illustrated, a hex map may be a good choice. Furthermore, in a multifaceted, interactive display, hex maps can be useful as filtering and navigation tools (e.g., select the state of

HEX-TILE MAP

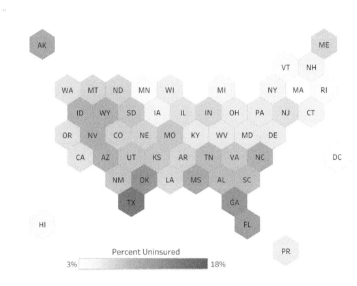

Data Source: Kaiser Family Foundation, Health Insurance Coverage of the Total Population, 2018 | Visual: HDV

FIGURE 7.4   Hex-tile map.

interest and all of the charts on display will change to display the selected state's data). Their use must be considered carefully, however, as they cannot be applied at all geographic levels (e.g., by country, region, county, ZIP code, census tract), and their geometric shape can obscure true regional variation.

Symbol/Dot-Density Maps

Symbol/dot-density maps place a dot at the geographic location of each event or measure of interest. Perhaps one of the most famous examples of this type of map was created by Dr. John Snow when he was investigating a cholera outbreak in London in the 1850s. Snow took the data shown in the table in Figure 7.5 (excerpt on the left) and created the density map shown on the right, which has a mark for the location of each cholera death. Each line on Snow's map represents a death: the density of the marks corresponds to the frequency of the event. Visualizing the data in this way revealed that the cholera deaths were clustered around the Broad Street water pump. Keep in mind this was at a time when people did not understand disease transmission, and the "miasma" theory (in the atmosphere) was the prevailing school of thought. Nonetheless, Snow's map persuaded authorities to remove the handle from the contaminated water pump, and cholera deaths declined. Snow's data display is a powerful example displaying the correct data in a meaningful way to inform action.

Dr. John Snow's Symbol/Dot-Density Map of Cholera Deaths

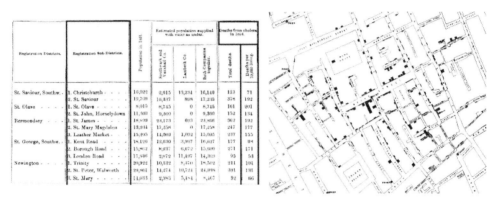

Sources: http://johnsnow.matrix.msu.edu/images/online_companion/chapter_images/fig10-4.jpg
http://matrix.msu.edu/~johnsnow/images/online_companion/chapter_images/fig12-5.jpg

FIGURE 7.5   Dr. John Snow's symbol/dot-density map of cholera deaths. *Sources:* http://johnsnow.matrix.msu.edu/images/online_companion/chapter_images/fig10-4.jpg http://matrix.msu.edu/~johnsnow/images/online_companion/chapter_images/fig12-5.jpg.

In symbol/dot-density maps, dots can have a one-to-one or one-to-many ratio with the measure. For instance, one dot could be mapped for each hospital in the United States (one-to-one) or, representing 1,000 births in each ZIP code, to geographic variations in fertility rates (one-to-many). Similar to choropleth maps, dot-density maps are intuitive and easy to interpret. However, they provide only at-a-glance glimpses into geographic variations in the data, without allowing viewers to easily access and compare numbers such as rates or counts across regions.

Proportional Symbol Maps

Symbol maps are dot-density maps where the size of the dots varies according to a measure. Consider the first map in Figure 7.6, which shows hospitals by their ZIP code.

Each dot is sized according to the number of hospitals in that ZIP code. Slight transparency allows the viewer to see density where dots overlap. This map type can be useful if the viewer is interested in details of specific locations. However, because hospital density correlates with population density, creating a choropleth map shaded by the number of hospitals per 100,000 people might be a better way to

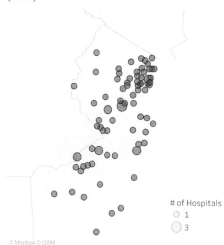

⊘ PROPORTIONAL SYMBOL MAP

Number of Hospitals by ZIP Code in New Jersey (2018)

# of Hospitals
○ 1
◯ 3

© Mapbox © OSM

- Can see more precise location data
- Hard to make meaningful inferences from bubble size
- Bubbles overlap and obscure one another
- Hard to identify areas needing attention

⊘ NORMALIZED CHOROPLETH MAP

Number of Hospitals per 100,000 People in New Jersey by County (2018)

© Mapbox © OSM

Number of hospitals per 100,000 people

2.3 ▭▬ 8.4

- Normalized metric easier to compare across geographies
- Sequential color palette allows user to easily identify areas with high or low hospital density

Data Sources: Medicare.gov and U.S. Census Bureau | Visual: HDV

FIGURE 7.6 Proportional symbol map vs. choropleth map.

identify provider-shortage areas, for instance. It is also useful to recall that, for reasons covered in Chapter 8, users have difficulty meaningfully assessing and comparing dots (or bubbles) of different sizes.

Also, as described in Chapter 6, dots (points) may be overlaid on a choropleth map to display information such as population density (map color saturation) along with a dot (point) to indicate the location of a hospital or treatment clinic (for example).

When Not to Use a Map

Just because geographic data can be displayed as a map does not necessarily mean it should be. Maps are limited in specific ways when presenting geographic data: they do not allow for sorting, ranking,

CHOROPLETH MAP

Percent of People without Health Insurance by State (**2018** vs. **2017**)

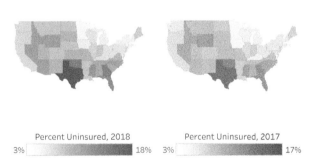

- Great for seeing geographic variations
- Easy to interpet at a glance, even at granular levels (such as by ZIP Code or Census Track)
- Cannot sort or rank
- Cannot limit to "Top N" to frame a story
- Difficult to add comparison data in a meaningful way

BAR CHART

Top 10 States for the Percent of People without Health Insurance in 2018, Compared to **2017**

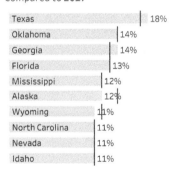

- Can sort and rank
- Can limit to "Top N" to frame a story
- Can add reference lines with comparison data
- Cannot see geographic variations
- May not be useful for very granular geographic data (such as ZIP Codes or Census Tracks)

Data Source: Kaiser Family Foundation, Health Insurance Coverage of the Total Population, 2018 | Visual: HDV

FIGURE 7.7 Use maps carefully.

top/bottom N analysis, or adding contextual information such as reference values. If it is more important for the user to gain these types of insights than to see geographic variations, the geographic data may be more effectively displayed using visualization methods described elsewhere in this book. Take, for example, the choropleth map in Figure 7.1. If instead of seeing geographic variations, a user was more interested in seeing the states with the highest uninsured rates and how they compare to the prior year, a sorted bar chart with reference lines would be a better display (Figure 7.7).

Summary

This chapter includes an overview of the four map types most common and useful for displaying health and healthcare data, and key considerations when using them. There are additional types of data maps and sophisticated mapping tools (such as ArcGIS) that can create highly detailed, dynamic, and robust geographic visualizations. For a deeper dive into mapping, we recommend checking out the resources provided at the end of this book.

Chapter Eight

Graphs and Charts to Never Use or Use with Caution

When "Cool Displays" Are Anything But

We all aspire to create displays of exceedingly complex health and healthcare data that are elegantly simple, powerfully informative, and memorable for the stories they reveal. Nevertheless, all too often, viewers request, and some visualizers are delighted to create, complicated and seemingly "cool" charts that only make data more difficult to comprehend and remember.

One reason people love "cool" graphs and charts (for which data visualization pioneer Edward Tufte coined the term "chartjunk") may be a function in part of biology. Humans are naturally programmed to feel a positive connection to specific shapes, such as circles, as well as new and exciting visual objects ("Look, something shiny!"). However, regardless of what may be an innate tendency, it is the job of health and healthcare and data visualization experts to steer people toward the most useful charts—those that, according to current research, communicate in an understandable, explainable, and actionable manner—rather than the most attractive ones.

Simple lack of training and awareness of why a particular chart is ineffective at communicating information may also make users susceptible to it. As covered in Chapter 4, the best practices of data visualization are not intuitive—they have been developed over time based on principles of human vision and cognition that must be studied and learned.

Those who create "cool" displays with lots of shiny accoutrements sometimes claim they do so to make them "memorable"—that is, attention-grabbing. Otherwise, proponents argue, no one will even look at them. They contend that once engaged by the frills, viewers will actually invest time in trying to figure out the display. But this justification for creating unnecessarily complicated, bad displays has no reliable research to support it; moreover, as described in Chapter 4, a wealth of credible research supports just the opposite.

This does not mean that displays should not be attractive, beautiful, and sometimes even fun. Whenever possible and appropriate—and with allowances for the purpose of the display—they should be. But designs with such attributes must not be confused with chartjunk. If the graph or chart used to display data is not in alignment with the best practices of data visualization, it will ultimately fail and nothing of importance will be conveyed or remembered.

> "The essential test of design is how well it assists the understanding of the content, not how stylish it is."
> —*Edward Tufte*

This chapter reviews examples of various charts that should never be used, or used only with extreme caution in unusual, very specific circumstances.

For each display type, there is an example of what not to do and why, alongside the more effective alternative chart type. This format offers readers the tools and explanations to justify, even defend, the selection or rejection of a particular chart type: why the more complicated one is not ideal; when it could be used (if ever); and what alternative visual display would be preferable, based on best practice.

Charts that should be used with caution and only in specific situations are indicated with an exclamation point; charts to never use are marked with an X; correctly used alternatives have a checkmark (Figure 8.1).

Never Use   Use With Caution   Best Practice

FIGURE 8.1   Icons are used to indicate graphs and charts to never use or use with caution, and the best practice choice.

Pie and Donut Charts

Why People Use Them

Circles can be found everywhere in the natural world. A short walk outside presents us with numerous round objects: an acorn, a sea-urchin shell, ladybug, or pebble. The Sun, a full moon, a drop of dew on a blade of grass are all circular. Three of the oldest circle archetypes—spiral, sectioned, and concentric circles—were drawn by prehistoric humans around the world. Evidence abounds that humans' love for circles has both evolutionary and historical origins. It may be, therefore, that human DNA is simply built to find the circular shape of a pie or a donut chart attractive. However, what humans like does not always equal the best design to communicate complex health and healthcare data.

Characteristics

A key requirement of a pie chart is that all the parts of the whole are visualized. On a pie chart, the slices divide the circle: for example, 50% of the pie would take up 180° (out of 360°) of the display.

One task a pie chart may be useful for is introducing young children to simple fractions such as 1/2 or 1/4. Occasionally, and when they are limited to no more than a couple of slices, they may also be useful for the display of simple proportional information on maps, such as the percent of men versus women in each state.

A donut chart is simply a pie chart with a hole in the middle. Donut charts were developed as a creative alternative to the pie to provide a more minimalist design with less ink, as well as to open a space in the center of the circle for text or large numbers.

Donut charts tend to draw the viewer's attention, as they are creative and sleek, but do not be fooled: they are just pie charts in disguise.

Challenges

Despite the seeming simplicity of pie and donut charts, recognized data visualization experts (including the authors of this book) caution against their use for highly rational and defensible reasons.

Pie and donut charts require the interpretation of angles, arc length, and areas in a circle, and the translation of them into a percentage or proportion of the circle's area. It is known, however, that humans are not very good at assigning accurate values to any of these, and they are even worse at translating them into a percentage (Kosara, 2016) This fact is supported by studies showing that when groups of people are asked to guess the values of the different slices of a pie chart, the results vary dramatically. The task becomes even more difficult for people when the different slices are close in value but far away from each other on the chart.

Pie and donut charts also use different colors to encode each value being displayed, which almost always requires a separate legend. This arrangement forces viewers to look back and forth from the legend to the chart while trying to remember which color goes with which value, thereby taxing their short-term memory and hindering insights about the actual data. Further, legends take up precious visual display real estate that could be put to better use.

Pie and donut charts have several other limitations that make them poor choices to display important health and healthcare data. They cannot support ranking of values; comparison values cannot be included in any clear or meaningful way; additional contextual information (e.g., trendlines or figures and icons representing changes in the values) cannot be arranged near the different values on more complex displays such as dashboards.

Moreover, although some advocate their use because they "add up to 100%," this is both a dangerous line of reasoning and insufficiently compelling. As discussed in Chapter 6 in the section on "challenging the 100% Myth," if the underlying data does not add up to 100%, it is still possible to create these types of charts. Therefore, this is also not a compelling argument for their use.

As American mathematician John Wilder Tukey (1915–2000) said, "There is no data that can be displayed in a pie chart that cannot be displayed better in some other type of chart." The following section shows what that better chart almost always is.

Best Practice Alternative

Because of the challenges described above, bar charts are virtually always preferable to pie or donut charts (Figure 8.2).

Bar charts encode values by the length of the bar, which lends itself easily to visual interpretation. For example, by merely comparing bars to each other and a scale, viewers can confidently grasp their proportionality. Further, bar charts can be labeled directly, thereby eliminating the need for a legend.

Bar charts may be ranked from high to low or vice versa. Reference lines can be added to provide additional context that cannot be placed in a pie or donut chart. Displays can be limited to a specific focus, such as "top ten results." Finally, additional contextual information such as a trendline graph or a figure describing a change in value from one point in time to another may be placed before or after a bar chart in a single row. Not one of the clarifying or supportive methods named here can be used with a pie or donut chart. (For more examples of the versatility of bar charts, refer to Chapter 6.)

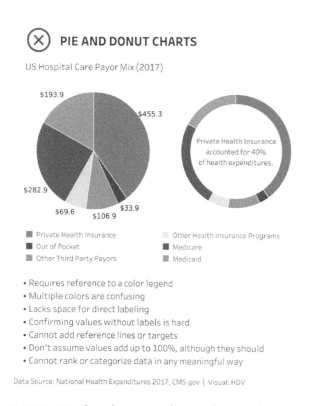

FIGURE 8.2 Bar charts are always a better choice than pies or donuts.

Multiples of Several-Part Stacked Bar Charts (MSPSBCs)

Why People Use Them

The title of this section is as complicated and multi-part as is the type of data display it describes: "multiples" (two or more) of "several-part" (three or more) "stacked" (having many parts close to each other) bar charts. This type of display might be used to show, for example, total enrollment in five different insurance plans (one bar for each plan), by three or more different age groups within each plan's bar.

Multiples of several-part stacked bar charts (MSPSBCs) might be popular because they are easy to create—or perhaps because of their bright colors. It is more likely, however, that designers and viewers simply have not discovered other, more effective techniques to show several categories of data in total, and (simultaneously) their respective sub-categorical values.

Characteristics

Stacked bar charts are designed to display the total value of a metric, and to quantify the parts contributing to the whole. The overall length of the bar represents the total; the subcategories are displayed using different colors within each bar. For example, different medical conditions and payor type; enrollees in different insurance plans by age group; types of medication errors by cause; monthly HIV prep screenings by public health district. When used to compare only two subcategories of data (such as male vs. female), or at most three, in each unique bar, they can be effective. However, they become incomprehensible when more than two or three subcategories of data are displayed within each bar.

Challenges

Although they may seem like the only possible solution, MSPSBC graphics do not in fact solve the challenge of comparing lots of categories and subcategories of health and healthcare data. The inherent problem with any bar chart containing more than two parts is that subsequent parts begin and end at different places on the scale, resulting in the need for workarounds for deciphering them. One such workaround is when the value of each part is labeled directly (not always feasible due to space constraints), resulting in a multicolored table of different-sized cells. Another workaround may be that viewers try to perform mental gymnastics in an attempt to calculate, and then hold in short-term memory, each part's value and its associated color. This results only in an overtaxed memory and a frustrated viewer. Regardless of the final workaround, attempting to compare all of this information across and between multiple several-part stacked bars can feel like a psychedelic trip, ending with a headache—and no valuable insights.

For example, Figure 8.3 shows the total enrollment in clinical trials for ten different pharmaceutical companies. It is easy to see that overall, GlaxoSmithKline (GSK) has the largest number of enrollments during the period, but some mental calculations have to be done to determine the exact number. In the same bar, it is also almost impossible to quickly understand the values of the small yellow segment representing the clinical trials that are active but not recruiting, and to accurately compare them across pharmaceutical companies. What about those that are currently recruiting? Does Merck or Pfizer have more in recruitment? Again, the MSPSBC fails here: it is not designed to compare, rank, or evaluate subcategories relative to one another.

The stacked bar chart even used correctly to display two, and on rare occasions, three parts, may still have the inconvenient and complicating requirement of multiple colors to encode different values. Along with its other drawbacks, this feature necessitates a legend.

Legends create extra work for users, who will be required to match color to subcategory for each one displayed. Additionally, as in the example in Figure 8.3, smaller subcategories become very difficult

MULTIPLE STACKED BARS

Clinical Trial Enrollment
by Pharmaceutical Company and Trial Status (1984-2020)

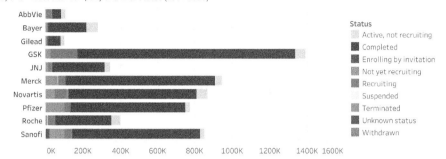

- Unable to accurately compare each segment of the stacked bar across dimensions
- Requires the use of a color legend and individual segments cannot all be labeled
- Values on the third and any subsequent part must be calculated by the viewer because they begin and end on random places of the scale
- On rare occasion, may be useful to provide a general sense of 3 to 4 parts that comprise the whole

 SMALL MULTIPLE BAR CHART

Clinical Trial Enrollment
by Pharmaceutical Company and Trial Status (1984-2020)

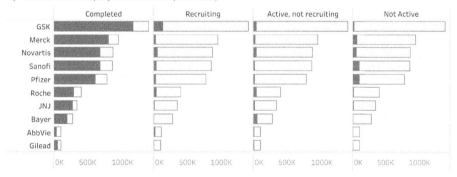

- Able to compare values across rows and down columns
- Only one color is necessary, as rows and columns separate dimensional values
- Space available to label all bars if necessary
- Can add meaningful context such as reference lines

Data Source: Harvard Dataverse - https://dataverse.harvard.edu/dataset.xhtml?persistentId=doi:10.7910/DVN/S8C77Q | Visual: HDV

FIGURE 8.3   Small multiple bar charts are a better alternative to multiple part stacked bars.

to distinguish when squished in a multiple stacked bar chart. Try identifying which pharmaceutical companies have values for "Not yet recruiting."

Best Practice Alternative

Fortunately, there is an excellent alternative to the MSPSBC: a small multiple bar chart. This chart organizes subcategories into columns (Figure 8.3), allowing for easy comparisons across categories and within a subcategory. By adding a shaded "total" bar behind each bar's value, we can also compare the subcategory's value to the overall one, thereby providing a visual percent of the total analysis. Only a single overall color is needed to interpret this visual; therefore, no color legend is required because headers distinguish each row and column. Even with the small values of some subcategories, there is space to label all values if needed, which was not an option in the multiple stacked bar chart.

Bubble Charts

Why People Use Them

What is there not to love about bubbles? As with pie and donut charts, bubble charts feature figures whose rounded borders are more naturally pleasing than those of sharper-edged shapes like squares or triangles.

It is also probably true that bubble charts have proliferated in the visual landscape because they are offered as an "out-of-the-box" chart solution in data visualization applications. Bubbles are prominently featured as a "simple" chart-design solution; they're pretty; everyone recognizes them. As a result, people who have not been trained in the best practices of data visualization are enticed into using (and misusing) them to try for a striking, memorable visual representation of data, or to add pizzazz to a dashboard.

Characteristics

The packed bubble chart visualizes one or more categorical variable[s] or dimension[s], such as country, and one quantitative variable or measure encoded in size, such as population. Color can be used to add a third quantitative variable, such as vaccine coverage rates, as shown in the example in Figure 8.4. The bubbles are not plotted on coordinates, but instead are packed together.

A cartogram, or bubble map, and a sized scatterplot both plot points on the x and y (latitude and longitude or two distinct measures) coordinates to display data. In addition to the two plotted variables, a third variable is indicated by the size of the bubble.

In Figure 8.4, the sized scatterplot shows countries by vaccine coverage rate and GDP per capita. The size of each bubble represents that country's population. All bubble charts use the area of the circle to represent an additional measure, often a third variable that cannot otherwise be plotted on the graph. The size gives additional context about the data variable in the visual display. This display can be useful in providing an overview of three variables and their relationship. In the example in Figure 8.4 (top right), the relationship between the two variables is clear: as GDP per capita increases, so does the vaccine coverage rate. This chart also is effective in identifying outliers: for example, in Figure 8.4, the country of Ukraine, which has a small population and a relatively high per-capita GDP, nevertheless has a low vaccine coverage rate.

Challenges

Packed bubble charts should never be used for the following reasons: humans are notoriously bad at determining the area of a circle and making *accurate* comparisons between circles of various sizes. For example, in Figure 8.4, look at the large circle representing the United States: population, 320 million. Now look at the bubble for Indonesia and try to accurately determine its population. Perhaps you guessed around 300 million (258 million is correct).

Additionally, because the packed bubbles are jumbled together, viewers cannot accurately compare values, especially for circles not in very close proximity. Further, the data as presented cannot be ranked or displayed in any other logical order.

Labeling is almost impossible in this display, especially on the smaller circles, which leaves exact values tucked away and covered over. Even an interactive hover feature (if available) fails to make this an effective chart, because it is both tedious and taxing for the viewer to try to hold all of the detailed information in short-term memory.

Sized scatterplots have their benefits, but as with any scatterplot, the risk that the data values on them will overlap and muddle or hide one another is greatly increased due to the bubbles of various sizes. As with the packed bubble chart, direct labeling is not possible on all bubbles, and the viewer will not be able to quickly or confidently grasp what dimension each bubble represents.

Best Practice Alternative

A fantastic alternative to bubbles is the table lens (or matrix of bar charts). A table lens is a display designed specifically to visualize large quantities of information across multiple metrics with different axes values such as count, rate, currency. The table lens uses a row/column format to visualize three or more variables across a common categorical variable, resulting in a series of side-by-side horizontal bars. The rows of data being displayed in the columns have one direct label applied in the column furthest to the left, followed by the bars in each category, which are aligned with how many people read.

For the purpose of a visual example, the table lens chart in Figure 8.4 shows a subset of countries and the corresponding values for three metrics: vaccine coverage rate, population, and GDP per capita. While this view is limited to the top-ten countries with the lowest vaccine coverage rates, a table lens is very effective at visualizing a much larger number of categorical variables across multiple quantitative variables. Another advantage of a table lens is the ability to sort according to each category of variables to explore results (that is, whichever row is selected for the primary sort order causes the other columns to align their values accordingly).

PACKED BUBBLES

Population and Vaccine Coverage, by Country
Size = 2015 Population; Color = Vaccine Coverage %

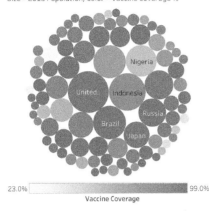

23.0% ▭ 99.0%

Vaccine Coverage

- Cannot accurately determine value by radius/area
- Cannot accurately describe or compare values displayed by size and color
- Cannot directly label or include additional contextual data
- Interactive hovering to view values taxes our short-term memory
- No ability to sort in a meaningful way

SIZED BUBBLE SCATTERPLOT

Vaccine Coverage and GDP per Capita, by Country
Size = 2015 Population

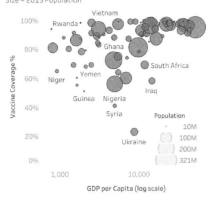

GDP per Capita (log scale)

- Shows correlation and outliers well
- Can visualize many data points
- Bubbles often overlap and obfuscate one another
- Hard to make comparisons for a single measure
- Cannot directly label all bubbles
- Interactive hovering to view values taxes our short-term memory
- Requires a size legend that can be difficult to match

TABLE LENS

10 Countries with the Lowest Vaccination Rates
Compared to 2015 Population and GDP per Capita

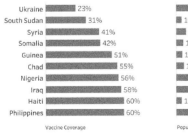

	Vaccine Coverage	Population	GDP per Capita
Ukraine	23%	44.9M	$8,762
South Sudan	31%	10.7M	
Syria	41%	18.0M	$4,956
Somalia	42%	13.8M	
Guinea	51%	11.4M	$2,034
Chad	55%	14.1M	$1,651
Nigeria	56%	181.1M	$4,966
Iraq	58%	35.6M	$14,663
Haiti	60%	10.7M	$1,649
Philippines	60%	102.1M	$6,825

- Able to meaningfully sort and rank values
- Can easily compare across multiple measures
- Can compare within a single measure
- Can show all values or a subset to frame a story
- Can add reference lines or target lines
- Can label values plus additional data context

Data Source: WHO and UNICEF; Gapminder; GGDC - sourced from OurWorldInData.org | Visual: HDV

FIGURE 8.4 Table lens displays are a better alternative to packed bubbles. Use sized bubble scatterplots with caution.

Treemaps

Why People Use Them

As previously noted, most visualization applications provide on-demand chart types that users can simply click and produce in a matter of seconds. The real problem this creates is that although these charts look fun and sophisticated, or seem a logical choice, they often are far more complicated than is needed, or have other flaws that make them the absolute wrong choice.

Treemaps are used (far too often!) as an alternative to a pie or donut chart and, most egregiously, to the correct choice, a bar chart. Additionally, while treemaps do seem to provide a solution for displaying parts-to-whole data, they are not designed to display only one "level" of data, as shown in Figure 8.5. Instead, they are specifically designed to display complex hierarchical data.

 **TREEMAP**

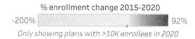

Medicare Advantage Enrollment by Organization in 2020
Color indicates percent change from 2015 enrollment

% enrollment change 2015-2020
-200% ▭ 92%
Only showing plans with >10K enrollees in 2020

| UnitedHealth Group, Inc. | Humana Inc. | CIGNA |
| CVS Health Corporation | WellCare Health Plans, Inc. | Rite |

- Designed to show hierarchies of data, not single categories or dimensions that are better displayed in a bar chart
- Unable to label all boxes directly, particularly smaller ones
- Cannot be ranked or ordered in any other logical manner

Data Source: CMS.gov - https://www.cms.gov/Research-Statistics-Data-and-System/Statistics-Trends-and-Reports/MCRAdvPartDEnrolData/Monthly-Enrollment-by-Contract

FIGURE 8.5 Treemaps are designed to show hierarchical data, not single dimensions that are better displayed in bar charts.

Characteristics

In the 1990s, Ben Shneiderman of the University of Maryland imagined a new technique for displaying space-constrained visualizations of hierarchies—or alternatively, and more simply, to visualize large quantities of hierarchical data, far too numerous to be displayed directly and effectively in a bar graph.

The entire rectangular treemap visualization represents the whole (the highest level of the hierarchy). The next is the secondary level within the categorical hierarchy. This level is represented as the larger rectangles within the complete visualization. Within these rectangles are many smaller ones that represent the hierarchy's third level.

The size of each rectangle corresponds to the size of the value being displayed. Using different saturations of colors encodes yet another value, such as year-over-year change, percent increase or decrease from a target, or another value not being represented by comparative size.

Challenges

Treemaps are a relatively complicated type of visualization technique designed to solve the challenge of how to display multiple categories and subcategories (hierarchies) of data. The mistake most often seen, however, is that the displays of health and healthcare data in a treemap do not present the same challenges.

For example, in Figure 8.5 of just one category of Medicare Advantage Plan Enrollment by Payor Group, a treemap is a poor choice of chart type. Instead, a bar chart should be used.

In the treemap shown in Figure 8.6, a hierarchy of data is being displayed, which is the correct use of this type of chart. The whole display is the Medicare Advantage Plan Enrollment. At the next level, the different plan names are represented by rectangles.

Different saturations of color display the percent change (darker = increased, lighter = decreased) in enrollment counts from 2015 to 2020. The plans represented by tiny rectangles are too small to label and can be interpreted only in an interactive visual where labels are available upon a hover action. As a result, larger sections of the treemap may have enough space for a label, but smaller ones do not.

Although the second treemap is an example of its correct usage, it still has limitations. If viewers need to see and compare each plan's details, a treemap may not be the best solution. For example, under the parent organization United Health Group, Inc., it is clear that one plan has the majority of enrollees, but unclear what the exact values are. And there is no easy way to make comparisons between plans or rank them in any meaningful way.

Best Practice Alternative

As is evident by now, bar charts are the powerhouses of data visualization, and can be used in a multitude of ways depending on the data to be displayed. The bottom chart in Figure 8.6 shows a bar chart of the parent organizations that administer Medicaid Advantage plans (limited in this instance to the top five, due to space constraints of this book). Using bars allows for reference lines to be added, to show directly the values of a comparison year (or target value), thereby providing a more precise interpretation of how much change has occurred.

In order to display the hierarchical level of detail, an accompanying bar chart showing the subcategory details (plan name, in this example) may be created and linked electronically as a drill-down, or included as another chart in a paper report.

In Figure 8.6, the bottom chart to the right shows the exact enrollment values for each plan within WellCare Health Plans, Inc. (for example). Additionally, reference lines and colors show exact changes in enrollment counts, and the plans can be ranked and sorted in a meaningful order. There is adequate space to add labels for direct details, or they can be available upon hover in interactive displays.

TREEMAP

Medicare Advantage Enrollment by Plan in 2020
Color indicates percent change from 2015 enrollment

% enrollment change 2015-2020
-240% ▭ 98%
Showing only plans with >10K enrollees in 2020

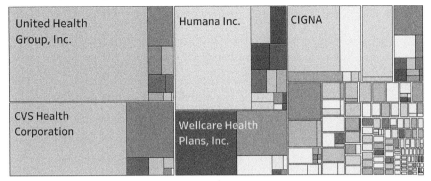

- Visualizes a large amount of hierarchical information in a compact space
- Works well in an interactive display, but difficult to understand in a static image
- Utilizes spatial grouping to show hierarchy effectively, but loses value with too many groups
- Unable to label most values and analyzing relationships or comparisons of size is impossible

✓ **BAR CHART WITH ASSOCIATED DRILL-DOWN**

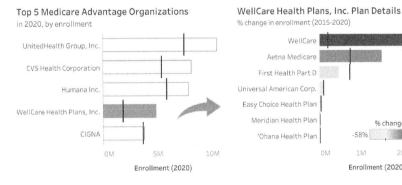

- Bars allow for easy comparison of actual values and may be ranked or sorted in some other logical way
- Can add reference lines for comparisons or context, which is not possible on a treemap
- While a bar chart of all hierarchical values would be quite lengthy, interactive displays allow for "expansion" of underlying details (lower levels in the hierarchy)
- Can directly label bars with headers and values

Data Source: CMS.gov - https://www.cms.gov/Research-Statistics-Data-and-Systems/Statistics-Trends-and-Reports/MCRAdvPartDEn-rolData/Monthly-Enrollment-by-Contract | Visual: HDV

FIGURE 8.6 Treemaps are complex displays of hierarchical data and must be used with caution. Whenever possible, use bar charts organized in clever ways to display the same data.

Marimekko (Mekko or Mosaic) Charts

Why People Use Them

The Marimekko (Mekko) chart got its name from the famous Finnish textile prints of predominantly abstract patterns in overlapping vibrant colors. Like the textiles, they can be bright and colorful and attractive to viewers—they have a bit of glamour. Further, like so many of the other charts described in this chapter, they have become much easier to create using data visualization software applications.

Characteristics

Also called a Mosaic chart, the Mekko chart visualizes two or more qualitative variables (yes/no, urban/suburban/rural, inpatient/outpatient) in a stacked, contiguous bar and a quantitative variable (total cost, length of stay, patient volume), either in a raw number or on a 0–100% normalized scale.

Mekko charts can be effective in showing parts-to-whole relationships across two categorical variables at once. They can also show the "weight" of a measure, or how large it is. Figure 8.7 shows waste-processing by country. The two categorical variables in this example are "country" and "waste-processing type" (recycling and composting, landfill). The quantitative variable is the percent of total waste processing by each processing type. The width of the bars represents the actual volume of waste in billions of kilograms.

For viewers trained to read a Mekko chart, the width of each bar helps to interpret the overall impact or "weight" of the normalized values. For example, Figure 8.7 shows that the United States has the most municipal waste at 238 billion kilograms, evidenced by the bar's width. The United States recycles or composts 35% of its waste, which is less than Denmark at 46%. However, Denmark is a smaller country and, as evidenced by the thin bar, does not produce much waste overall. Denmark's 46% recycling and composting is much smaller in raw values (2 billion kg) than is the case in the United States (83 billion kg).

MARIMEKKO CHART (MEKKO OR MOSAIC CHART)

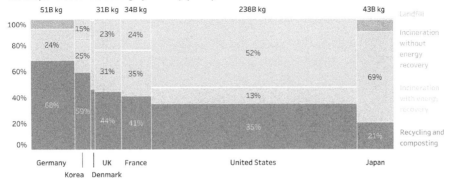

- Provides additional information on size
- Stacked bars make comparisons difficult
- Complicated for the average viewer
- Requires time to interpret the various encoding strategies (size, height, color)
- Labeling is challenging for small sections

 SMALL MULTIPLE BAR CHART WITH TOTALS

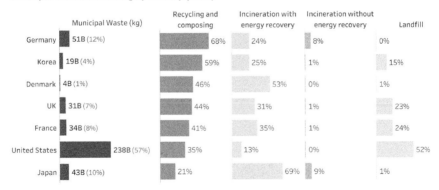

- Quickly gain insights across variables
- Can label all bars for exact values
- Can sort and rank variables
- Easy to make comparisons within a column and down rows
- Column for overall size adds context

Data Source: OECD.org | Visual: HDV

FIGURE 8.7 Marimekko charts may be difficult for a viewer to understand. A small-multiple bar chart is a better alternative.

Challenges

The main shortcoming of Mekko charts is they are not intuitive, often requiring some explanation to understand. This may present a stumbling block that will discourage, even lose a viewer, user, or stakeholder who has never seen this type of display before. As in a stacked bar chart, more than two parts can be hard to compare across the different categories being displayed in the chart, and what is being encoded by the width of the bar is not always clear. Labeling all parts of the chart presents the same problems as in MSPSBCs, described above.

Best Practice Alternative

A data visualizer's job is to make data easier to understand, and provide charts that help viewers make decisions and form impressions about the data quickly. The same story can be told here, but in a more straightforward (though still engaging) way by using a small-multiple bar chart with totals.

The lower half of Figure 8.7 shows a small-multiple bar chart where the percentages for each waste type have their column, but with the same axis range. This arrangement allows the viewer to make comparisons down and across the chart. A total column shown in the first column may be added to show denominators for all of the subsequent bars.

Radial Bar and Petal Charts

Why People Use Them

As is true with pie charts, donut charts, and packed bubbles, radial bar charts are often used in an attempt to make data more interesting. As stated earlier, some argue that when a visual display is unconventional, people will be more apt to engage with it and examine the data further because they are curious. Again, there is at present no reliable research to support this claim.

Also as previously described, people often tend to prefer circular objects to rigid ones with sharp edges; a radial bar chart may soften the feel of a regular bar chart. However, the visual twisting around a circle creates many more problems than it solves and, worse, will cause the viewer to misunderstand and misinterpret the data being displayed.

Characteristics

A radial bar chart is simply a bar chart plotted around a circle or on a polar coordinate plane, rather than on a rectangular, or Cartesian, plane. A radial bar chart can bend bars around the circumference of a circle (Figure 8.8, top left) or radiate bars outward from the center of a circle as in a petal chart (Figure 8.8, top right).

If radial bar charts are just regular bar charts shaped like circles, then why would anyone want to use them? Quite simply, they are used to add unnecessary excitement to a visualization because people mistakenly think that bar charts are boring. As discussed, and demonstrated throughout this book, bars are not boring—and what is more, they work. Furthermore, and to quote Steve Few, "Dressing up a chart in glitter and spangles to generate interest that does not exist in the information itself treats readers disrespectfully."

Challenges

The most significant problem with the radial bar chart is the "racetrack effect." On an actual racetrack, runners (for example) start at different places in their lanes to account for the fact that the outside lanes have a larger circumference and therefore are longer in actual distance than the inside lanes. For example, the runner on the outermost (ninth lane) starts ahead of the runner in the eighth lane, who starts ahead of the runner in the seventh lane, staggering the start points all the way to the runner in the first lane. This staggered starting place equalizes the distance around the track, and the runners can all end at the same finish line, having run the same distance.

This difference in circumference is not accounted for in a radial graph. There, all lanes are assumed to be equal in distance/value, as evidenced by the fact that they all have the same starting point. A radial graph simply takes a bar chart and bends it around a circle—but the effect of doing this is to obscure the real proportional differences between the actual values.

The example in Figure 8.8 shows how difficult it is to interpret radial bars and assign values accurately. The average length of stay (ALOS) for a patient in the Emergency Department who is to be admitted to psychiatry is 27.4 hours. Can you determine the ALOS value for pediatrics in the radial chart in Figure 8.8 (top left)?

A petal chart is also called a radial bar chart (even though it is different from the previous example); it has a center point with bars (petals) radiating outward. While the accuracy of the length of the petals is maintained, it becomes increasingly difficult to compare values that are not near each other. In the top right example in Figure 8.8, try to compare the values for neurology and orthopedics, which are on opposite sides of the circle. Without the labels, making any accurate comparisons would be impossible. And, as with many of the other charts discussed in this chapter, petals may not be ranked or arranged in any other meaningful order; and no comparison value or other contextual values can be added.

This petal chart may be nice to look at, but it should never be used for the display of crucial health and healthcare data. In the words of Edward Tufte, "Allowing artist-illustrators to control the design and content of statistical graphics is almost like allowing typographers to control the content, style, and editing of prose."

Best Practice Alternative

Both a bar chart and a deviation bar chart are best practice alternatives for radial charts. One of the challenges, present with radial charts, is how difficult it is to use them for making visual comparisons such as "the ALOS for neurology is half as long as that for psychiatry." On a standard bar chart—even without labels—viewers can clearly see this relationship. Unlike most radial charts, deviation bar charts can display both positive and negative values (Figure 8.8, bottom right). It is difficult (where not impossible) to do this in a radial chart.

RADIAL BAR CHART

Average Length of Stay (hours)
in the ED by Admitting Inpatient Service

27.4 hours

- Radial bar lengths are not proportional to their value due to increased circumference
- Outer rings take up more visual space than inner rings, exaggerating their importance
- Without axes, guesses at angles or cramped labels at the end of each bar is required

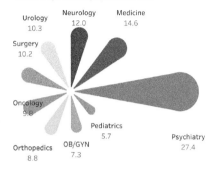 **PETAL CHART**

Average Length of Stay (hours)
in the ED by Admitting Inpatient Service

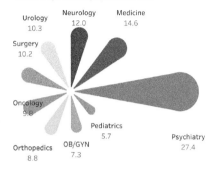

- Cannot easily compare values, especially on opposite sides of the circle
- Finite number of categories can be displayed
- Radial axes are difficult to add and interpret
- Cannot show negative values logically

 BAR CHART

Average Length of Stay (hours)
in the ED by Admitting Inpatient Service

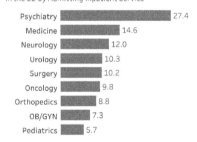

- Can sort and rank values
- Quickly can compare bar lengths
- Can make interpretations such as "The ALOS for Psychiatry is twice as long as that for Medicine" by comparing bar lengths

 DEVIATION BAR CHART

Expected ED Average Length of Stay (hours)
Difference from Observed
by Admitting Inpatient Service

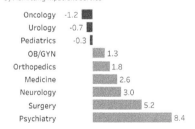

- Can sort and rank variables
- Can compare to (deviate from) a reference value
- Can show both positive and negative values
- Adequate space to label bars

Mock Data | Visual: HDV

FIGURE 8.8 Bar and deviation bar charts are always a best practice. Never use radial or petal charts.

Radar Charts

Why People Use Them

People use radar charts, sometimes called star or spider graphs, because the primary objective is to assess the symmetry of values versus their size. Radar charts can also be useful when the indicators to be displayed have different quantitative scales that may not be easily seen on a bar or other type of chart. Radar charts may also be chosen because their circular shape is appropriate for displaying circular data, that is, data measured on a circle in degrees or radians most often found in medical sciences and research fields. (On the circle, measurements at 0° and 360° represent the same direction, whereas on a linear scale they would be located at opposite ends of the scale.)

It must also be noted that it is not common to encounter the need for these types of displays. Therefore, it is more likely—as is true with so many of the charts described in this chapter—that radar charts are used because they are perceived as adding visual interest, not because they are the best choice for the job at hand.

Characteristics

As described above, a radar chart is circular with measures represented by axis lines that start in the center and extend to the outside edge of the display. In general, the axes scale is arranged with the lowest values in the center, increasing in value as they extend toward the circumference. The axis lines join each value, thereby forming a polygon, which is sometimes filled with color, as in the example in Figure 8.8 (left).

Challenges

Regardless of whether different or common scales are used to display values between axes on a radar chart, it is exceedingly difficult to compare values across radar charts, leading to errors in interpretation. Our human visual perception is hardwired to make comparisons on conventional displays of lines, points, and bars with relative ease. It is not, however, well adapted to focus on and figure out the curvatures, sweeps, and shapes displayed on radar charts.

Another challenge presented by this chart type is that the lines connecting the data may occlude (obstruct) one another as the values move closer together, or if they are identical. It's inevitable that when multiple series are plotted, some values will eventually be on top of and therefore blocking each other.

The area of the shapes presented increases as a square of the values, rather than linearly. This may cause viewers to misinterpret the data displayed, because a small difference in the values results in a significant change in the area, so the difference is visually exaggerated.

Although some people may like to use them or even claim to enjoy viewing them, radar charts are hard to understand and explain. They should be used only in unique and rare circumstances and for an audience that is expert in the data being displayed.

Best Practice Alternative

Encoding data on simple, easy-to-understand graphs using bars or points is the best practice alternative to radar charts. In the example in Figure 8.9 (right) a small multiple display with three different therapies (A, B, and C) is displayed in the columns and the outcomes of interest are displayed on the rows. At the bottom of the small multiple point chart is a bar chart, which summarizes the total score for the different therapies.

In this example, the small multiple point chart is designed to support an imagined shared decision-making conversation between a patient and doctor, where the different outcomes of interest and their efficacy may be compared and discussed through the lens of their utility (value) to the patient. For example, although Therapy A has the highest overall value score of 483 (displayed in the purple bar), if the patient highly values sexual function and lower urinary bother, he may choose Therapy B over A (A = 45 vs. B = 75 and A = 70 vs. B = 90, for sexual function and urinary bother respectively).

Data visualizations should be both easy to understand and easy to discuss. Given the choice of explaining the radar chart on the left versus the small multiples and bar charts to a patient facing a serious medical decision, which would you choose?

(X) **RADAR CHART**

Outcome Value Comparison for Prostate Cancer Treatments
Each category score 0-100 (100 = ideal); Not weighted for patient preference.

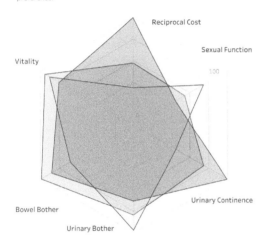

Individual Treatment Score Details

Therapy A   Therapy B   Therapy C

• Shape is arbitrary as it is dependent on the order of the metrics
• Unable to label all values and axes
• Radar shapes overlap, making distinguishing values difficult
• Many measures can leave the radar incomprehensible

(✓) **SMALL MULTIPLE POINTS**

Outcome Value Comparison for Prostate Cancer Treatments
Each category score 0-100 (100 = ideal); Not weighted for patient preference.

Outcome	Therapy A	Therapy B	Therapy C
Reciprocal Cost	100	35	58
Sexual Function	45	75	55
Urinary Continence	100	45	75
Urinary Bother	70	97	83
Bowel Bother	88	68	99
Vitality	80	90	95

Overall Outcome Value Scores
Max score = 600

Therapy A	483
Therapy B	410
Therapy C	465

• Can aggregate values such as overall score, and display in bars alongside a small multiple chart
• Small multiple points allow for comparison between treatment types, allowing viewers to consider potential tradeoffs
• Points can be labeled for accuracy

Mock Data | Visual: HDV

FIGURE 8.9   Radar charts are difficult to interpret. Small multiples and bar charts are the best practice alternative.

Sankey Diagrams

Why People Use Them

Because Sankey diagrams are complex and often colorful, they can tend to generate a lot of buzz and excitement. Unfortunately, because Sankeys can draw viewers' attention, people may use these trendy figures solely to have something visually attractive.

Characteristics

Sankey diagrams are named after Matthew Henry Phineas Riall Sankey, who in the late 1800s modified an earlier diagram to show the energy efficiency of a steam engine by illustrating the flow of steam. In linear Sankey diagrams, flow is represented from left to right by "bands," which vary in width proportional to the magnitude of the quantitative value represented (for example, patient count).

In healthcare, Sankey diagrams are most often used to show the flow of patients through a healthcare system. For example, in the top-right chart in Figure 8.10, overall discharge volume from each hospital is represented by the height of each sectioned bar on the far left. From there, bands flow from the hospital to the discharge physician, showing the volume of patients moving from point A to point B. The bars on the right represent the resulting proportion of patients seen by each physician after hospital discharge.

Sankeys support the display of complex processes, and can help a team make decisions about energy, time, pathways through a system, and capacity. However, as with all of the aforementioned chart types, a Sankey chart has a particular purpose, so while it looks captivating, it can be overly complicated and difficult for viewers to interpret.

Challenges

If there are many categories to display, the Sankey diagram can become a tangled mess of lines and colors. With many categories present, especially ones of small magnitude, following each line through the flow takes a lot of attention and effort. Ultimately, a poorly made Sankey can hide, rather than highlight, the actionable insights in the data.

The upper-left example in Figure 8.10 shows how tangled a Sankey can become when designed with a large number of categories.

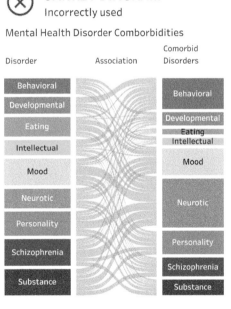

SANKEY DIAGRAM
Incorrectly used

Mental Health Disorder Comborbidities

- Excess of lines makes it incomprehensible
- Unable to label smaller sections
- Inaccurately showing associations between disorder and comorbid disorder, not flow

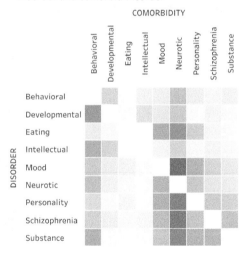

RELATIONSHIP MATRIX
showing association

Strength of Relationship Between Index Disorder and Comorbid Disorder

- Saturation = strength of relationship (value)
- Simple to compare within rows and columns
- Can sort and rank either rows or columns
- Color-coding each dimension is not needed

Data Sources: JAMA Psychiatry; Oleguer Plana-Ripoll, PhD; Carsten Bøcker Pedersen, DrMedSc; Yan Holtz, MSc; et al; Exploring Comorbidity within Mental Disorders Among a Danish National Population; https://jamanetwork.com/journals/jamapsychiatry/fullarticl.

FIGURE 8.10 Sankey charts are designed to show flow and should be used with caution.

SANKEY DIAGRAM
Correctly used

Patient Discharge Volume Flow from Hospital
to Receiving Physician

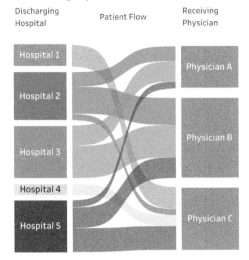

- Accurately showing flow of patients from
  hospital to physician
- Effective for a small number of categories
- Useful for high-level summary, not for details

HIGHLIGHT TABLE
with marginal histogram

Percent of Discharged Hospital Patients
Receiving Follow-Up Care by Physician

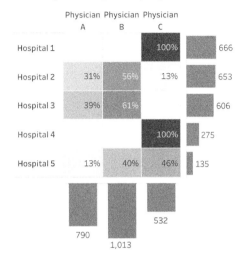

- Can show normalized percent or actual values
- Small space packs in many variables
- Quickly analyze where movement occurs
- Not limited to a certain number of dimensions

Data Sources: Mock Data | Visual: HDV

FIGURE 8.10 (Continued)

Sankeys use width to encode a quantitative variable, but because
the bands can move in front or behind one another, and up and
down, comparing the size of these bands is very challenging. The
segments on either end of the Sankey are essentially stacked bars
which, unless ranked by size, are difficult to compare (see this chapter's
previous section on Multiples of Several-Part Stacked Bar
Charts/MSPSBCs).

Lastly, the Sankey chart is widely misused when it displays relationship,
correlation, and parts-to-whole. For example, a Sankey is not

an appropriate visual display to show how various diseases break down by race. People do not "flow" from disease to race. In the example in the upper left of Figure 8.10, the display shows a disorder (e.g., behavioral disorder, eating disorder) and the associated comorbid disorders (what other disorders are likely associated with the primary disorder). The reason this display is not effective is that people, again, are not moving from one disorder to another. The data show the associations between disorders and where there may be a more significant correlation with having a comorbid disorder.

In summary: Sankey charts should never be used simply to add flair to a visual display. Data do not need to be dressed up. Let the dataset speak for itself in the most uncomplicated display appropriate for the context of the data.

Best Practice Alternative

One best practice alternative to display these types of associations is through a relationship matrix (Figure 8.10, top right), where each square shows the relative strength of the association of the two variables, in this case, between the primary disorder and the comorbid disorder. Color encodes the degree of the relationship: darker squares have a stronger correlation than lighter ones. In this visual, viewers can clearly and quickly identify insights such as that the presence of a mental disorder is strongly associated with having a behavioral or developmental disorder. There is a very strong relationship between mood disorders and neurotic disorders.

When showing flow is the goal of the visual display, another alternative to a Sankey diagram is a highlight table with marginal histograms (Figure 8.10, bottom right). Similar to the relationship matrix, the highlight table shows values at the intersection of two variables, such as Hospital and Physician. The display shows the percent of patients from each hospital that have gone to each available physician. Viewers can quickly see that 100% of the patients discharged from Hospital 1 followed up with Physician C. This gives us a relative understanding of the flow of patients, but what about the volume? The marginal histogram adds the additional context of the actual volume of patients. The right shows the volume of patients discharged from each hospital; the bottom, the volume of patients that followed up with each physician.

One More Thing: 3-D

Some data and images displayed in 3-D are fantastic. For example, MRI images of the brain are beautiful, and have helped advance research and medical care by light years.

However, this is not the type of data most health and healthcare professionals work with every day; this is not the information visualization designers are communicating. Rather, they work with quantitative data, upon which people rely to interpret research studies and make public policy, management, and patient-care decisions.

It is easy enough to see that 3-D displays do not depict information very accurately, but more difficult to understand why people persist in using them. A large part of the motivation for people to display data in this way is that they believe it looks sophisticated, and they wish to impress the viewer. But there may be another extraordinarily interesting reason contributing to this behavior.

In a 1999 study about how people decide to present data, researchers Tractinsky and Meyer asked study participants to choose the display best suited for conveying to viewers "what is going on." They found that participants preferred 2-D graphs as an aid to making decisions, both when they were making the decision themselves and when the graph was to be shown to others making the same decision.

The researchers also found that participants preferred to use 3-D graphs when they believed the data were unfavorable. Tractinsky and Meyer interpreted this preference as a kind of compensatory behavior in which the presenter tries to show that he or she is competent even in the face of unfavorable data. Could it be that people look for ways to "put lipstick on the proverbial pig" of bad data or results? Perhaps.

Here is the bottom line. Stay away from 3-D effects when creating graphs; they just do not work.

 3-Dimensional Charts (3-D)

 2-Dimensional Charts

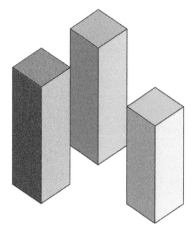

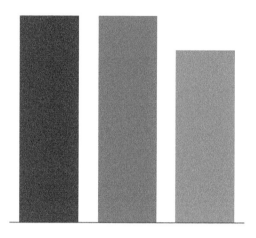

- Never apply 3-D effects to displays of quantitative data that only need 2 dimensionsn(2-D), and x- and y-axis
- Z-axis (the third dimension) distorts visual interpretation of graph's length, height, and width on all axes
- 3-D effects obfuscate parts of the overall display

- Quantitative data only requires 2 dimensions (2-D) to be easily understood
- Values are not obfuscated
- If viewers require more information, such as another dimension, consider techniques such as small multiple displays

Mock Data | Visual: HDV

FIGURE 8.11   Never use 3-D; 2-D is all that is needed and is the best practice.

Summary

If we focus only on the seemingly cool visualizations that many new software applications allow us to create easily—without understanding why they were conceived, what problems they are designed to solve, and the research behind how humans see and understand data and information—we run the risk of missing the bigger objective of creating clear, accurate, compelling views of crucial data.

However, if we commit to understanding the underlying structure of health and healthcare data and the best visualization to convey the meaning buried in it, we can create visualizations that people will be able to understand and explain—and that will lead to meaningful change in modern healthcare.

Chapter Nine

Making Accessible Visualizations

Accessible Design Is Good Design

In order to make health and healthcare data visualizations accessible to as broad an audience as possible, it is crucial to remember that some people may experience the visualizations differently than the way you envisioned. For instance, those with visual impairments or mobility limitations will experience the visualizations differently from those without such challenges. However, designing for accessibility is not predicated exclusively on the existence of a disabled or visually/physically limited audience. Components such as labels, text, white space, and colors crafted in a way that optimizes usability for everyone is the goal. Many of the methods for making data visualizations accessible are the same ones that simply make them good. Nevertheless, it is essential to design with particular human challenges and conditions in mind.

Accessibility in Data Visualization

Accessibility in data visualization is making the information in them usable for as many people as possible. As visualizations are being fine-tuned for accessibility, the delivery mode must always remain at the forefront of consideration. There are, for example, special considerations for web-based content. In the United States, the Americans with Disabilities Act (ADA) of 1990, and Section 508 of the Rehabilitation Act, require all web content—applications, websites, web pages and attached files such as PDFs—to be accessible to people with disabilities. The United States also has technical guidelines, called Web Content Accessibility Guidelines (WCAG), for meeting these requirements. Data products that will be publicly distributed online, especially those produced or published by a government or government-funded institution, are highly likely to have compliance required. Under any circumstances, makers committed to clear and compelling data visualizations know that maximizing accessibility is a crucial component of honoring this commitment.

It is helpful to think of the different ways people with and without disabilities consume visualizations. People who are blind, visually impaired, illiterate, or have learning disabilities often rely on screen-reading software to speak content out loud as they use the Tab key to navigate between components. Because screen-readers are purely an interpretive layer, there is no method to gather statistics on how many people use them. However, about 5.1% of U.S. American adults have significant difficulty seeing; 3.5% have a learning disability (census.gov). A user in this type of situation hears a web page explored one element at a time as the screen-reader describes both the content (written words) and functionality (a hyperlink, say) of each element. An image is not seen as an image; it is heard as a description that someone typed into the page's "Alt [alternative] text." If the web page is not designed for accessibility, the content may be narrated in an illogical or confusing order, leaving the user puzzled, lost, and deprived of a significant part of the value of the page. Additionally, 8% of men and 0.5% of women worldwide are colorblind (the common descriptor for someone with compromised ability to differentiate between colors), which restricts their ability to interpret the use of certain colors (as the signaling of heat, urgency, or danger by the color red) quickly and accurately.

People with mobility limitations may be able to see computer content, but do not have the fine motor capacity to use a mouse. (It is estimated that 5.6% of U.S. American adults have difficulty using their fingers to pick up a glass or grasp a pencil (census.gov)). They also rely on the Tab key for navigation. Tabbing is more accessible than clicking because the relatively slight movement of a single finger up and down (as opposed to the fine motor capacity of fingers, hands, and arms required for mouse control) suffices to operate the Tab key.

This chapter covers specific techniques to improve accessibility for the users described above, as well as ways to make visualizations more usable by everyone who depends on them.

Ways to Make Accessible Data Visualizations

- **Provide data as a text table.**

No matter how amazing a data visualization looks, visually impaired people do not take information in through sight. Therefore, they need access to data in another way, such as with a screen-reader, which says data values aloud to users. Screen-readers can read letters and numbers, but cannot always render charts or images. (Some software provides guidance as to which components are 508-compliant.) Providing text tables, data downloads, or both that are formatted to be readable by screen-readers and placing them in prominent locations on the screen allows quick, easy access and legibility.

- **Provide navigation and interaction components that can be controlled by both mouse and keyboard.**

Often, sophisticated data visualization software has interactivity options that may work only with mouse clicks—for instance, clicking one chart to filter another. To the extent possible, provide options for navigating between data elements or interacting with them (filtering; toggling between views) that work via a keyboard as well as a mouse. Options for navigation may need research into the capabilities of the software used, but those who rely on keyboard navigation will appreciate not getting stuck in an inoperable application. If non-accessible features provide significant value to the primary audience of a visualization, it is worthwhile to consider creating dashboard versions tailored to each audience (one accessible, one not).

- **Use colorblind-friendly and print-friendly colors.**

Chapter 4 of this book covers color and how people see. There are many reasons why color is not a trivial design decision; accessibility is one of them. Colorblindness (or color vision deficiency) affects approximately 1 in 12 men and 1 in 200 women worldwide—that is, approximately 300 million people, almost equal to the population of the United States. The most common type of color blindness is the inability to distinguish between reds and greens, but some people cannot tell blues from yellows, or even see any color at all.

When choosing a color to impart meaning, select palettes that are both colorblind- and printer-friendly so they are more likely to retain their meaning.

Some software applications have built-in colorblind palettes. Online resources can suggest the right colors and preview how they will look to people with various types of color blindness. (A list of resources comes at the end of this book.)

- **Use color and symbols together to impart meaning.**

Another way to improve accessibility is to use color plus a corresponding symbol in the same marker or display. That way, if users cannot distinguish between the colors, they can be guided by differences in the shapes (Figure 9.1).

USING COLOR AND SYMBOLS TOGETHER

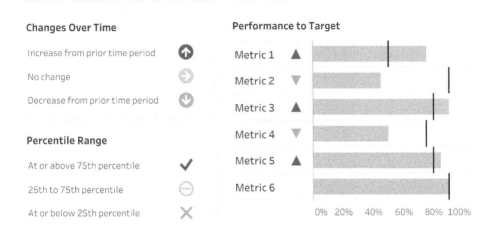

Mock Data | Visual: HDV

FIGURE 9.1   Use symbols and color to impart meaning.

- **Use adequate contrast.**

The ability to see falls on a spectrum. Some people have limited sight, and though they do not require a screen-reader, high contrast enhances their perception. Conversely, a text or chart element with low contrast to its background can be difficult to see. Text and chart elements must meet certain contrast ratio requirements to be judged accessible. Generally speaking, dark gray text on a white background is most legible, but other combinations also work: chart elements can be lighter than text; bolded text can be lighter than non-bolded. Contrast-checker websites (resources can be found at the end of this book) are useful for checking visualizations' contrast ratios and choosing appropriate colors. A best practice is to select color palettes with substantial contrast and color saturation variability between each color. (Chapter 4 covers color selection.)

- **Use clear, descriptive titles, captions, and "alt text."**

Many screen-readers cannot read chart elements but can read titles and captions. A clear, descriptive title helps all viewers understand a chart, but it is even more important to those who rely on screen-readers by providing information they may not be able to access in the chart. The right content for a title depends on the dissemination method for the visualization and its intended audience. For example, the title of a static report for the general public could include a key takeaway about the chart. The title of an interactive dashboard for an internal audience, in contrast, should concisely describe what the dashboard displays ("Hospital Length of Stay by Service").

Captions or "alt (short for alternative) text" can describe what is in the chart for the benefit of those who rely on screen-readers. Alt-text is associated with an image or graphical element that conveys the essential information of that image. It is a great way to add additional information for visually impaired users without needing to modify the visualization's components designed for fully sighted users.

- **Create legible, well-placed labels, legends, and footnotes.**

Clear, concise, easy-to-read labels are crucial to understanding data. Formatting choices like orientation, placement, and alignment can make them very effective, or much less so. Simply put: do not make the user work harder than is necessary.

Redundancy. A piece of information in a chart title need not be repeated in each label—repetitiveness and redundancy clutter the eye and the mind.

Orientation. It is often tempting to align text vertically to make labels fit better into an allotted space. However, this is typically not worth the sacrifice in legibility and accessibility. Turning the head (or the screen/page) to read a label, then turning it back to read values is fatiguing and time-consuming and hampers understanding. Instead, keep text horizontal, and reorient or re-space the data. (Chapter 6 provides more information about text orientation in charts.)

Placement. Labels and legends should be as close to their corresponding chart elements as is reasonable. Looking back and forth or scrolling up and down to identify what a label or legend corresponds to is extra work and forces users to rely heavily on short-term memory. It is worth recalling here the discussion of stacked bar charts in Chapters 6 and 8 of this book: cross-referencing between such a chart and its legend makes it particularly hard to read. When possible, eliminate the need for a legend by direct labeling (as is done with small multiples). Elements that begin on the bottom left of a chart or dashboard are likely to be overlooked, so avoid footnotes. Pack as much description into labels as possible instead.

Alignment. While there are no prescribed rules for text alignment in headers, labels, and titles, alignment is still an important consideration. Carefully aligning labels helps get them as close to their corresponding data as is reasonable (see the previous paragraph). Values displayed in tables should always be right-aligned to ensure the digits (1s, 10s, 100s, and so forth) are aligned and to help viewers easily compare their size. Right-aligning column headers as well help the eye associate the label with the value.

Conversely, left-aligning column headers in a small-multiples bar chart may make the most sense, so they line up with the starting point of each bar. Further, center-aligned titles, labels, and headers can be harder to read than left-aligned text, especially if the text is long. Changing alignment requires only a few keystrokes; applying one or two different options to the displayed text should quickly make it clear which one works best (Figure 9.2).

- **Choose fonts carefully.**

Choosing a font may seem like a trivial design decision; it is definitely not in any setting, but particularly when considering accessibility. Fonts vary widely in legibility (how easy they are to read), and sometimes the prettiest or most striking types are the hardest to make out, especially by the visually impaired.

The two main font categories are "serif" and "sans-serif." Serif fonts have tiny horizontal lines/marks (called serifs) that lead the eye from

UNCLEAR TITLE AND LABELS   ✓ **CLEAR TITLE AND LABELS**

Insurance by state (excerpt)

	Employer based health insurance	Non-group private health insurance	Medicaid health insurance	Medicare health insurance	No health insurance	Other public health insurance
Alabama	46%	6%	21%	16%	10%	2%
Alaska	45%	3%	22%	9%	14%	7%
Arizona	45%	6%	22%	15%	10%	2%
Arkansas	42%	6%	27%	16%	8%	2%
California	47%	7%	26%	11%	7%	1%
Colorado	51%	8%	20%	12%	8%	2%

Percent of residents with each type of health insurance coverage by state (excerpt)

	Employer	Non-group private	Medicaid	Medicare	Other public	Not insured
Alabama	46%	6%	21%	16%	2%	10%
Alaska	45%	3%	22%	9%	7%	14%
Arizona	45%	6%	22%	15%	2%	10%
Arkansas	42%	6%	27%	16%	2%	8%
California	47%	7%	26%	11%	1%	7%
Colorado	51%	8%	20%	12%	2%	8%

- Vague title
- Column headers are vertical and repetitive
- Values and column headers are center-aligned
- Row headers are centered

- Clear, descriptive title
- Column labels are horizontal and not repetitive
- Values and column headers are right-aligned
- Row headers are left-aligned

Data Source: Kaiser Family Foundation Health Insurance Coverage of the Total Population, 2018 | Visual: HDV

FIGURE 9.2 Align labels horizontally to ensure they can be read.

one letter to the next so that they appear connected. Fonts with serifs are intended for sequences of words that exceed one line. Sans-serif (*sans* means "without" in French) fonts do not have the marks and are simpler and easier to read at a glance, making them the more appropriate choice for most data products.

Another characteristic to consider when choosing a font is the width assigned to each letter or character. Proportional typefaces assign varying widths to each letter or character based on its shape. (An *i* is allowed less space than a *w*.)

Non-proportional (monospaced) fonts allot each character, letter, and number the same amount of space. Monospaced fonts can be harder to read in a block of text, but their equal spacing makes them the only choice for ensuring that the numbers in lists, columns, and tables are aligned. A selection of serif and sans-serif fonts considered both legible and accessible includes Arial, Calibri, Times New Roman, Verdana, Helvetica, and Tahoma. (See Figures 9.3 and 9.4.)

FIGURE 9.3   Choose fonts carefully.

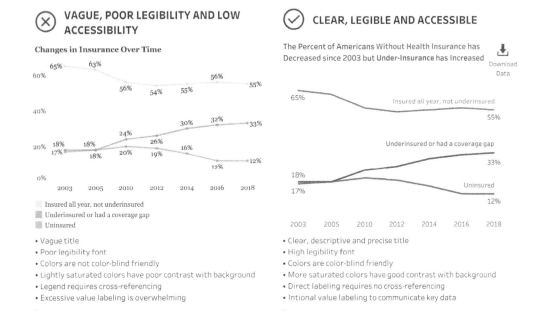

FIGURE 9.4   Label charts and graphs clearly and directly.

Summary

It is not possible to design a data visualization accessible to every single person who may encounter it, and that is okay. Techniques described in this chapter and provided throughout this book are excellent tools for creating clear, engaging data visualizations accessible to as many people as possible.

Creating Compelling Data Displays

"The greatest value of a picture is when it forces us to notice what we never expected to see."

—*John W. Tukey,*
Exploratory Data Analysis

Chapter Ten

Dashboards, Reports, and Multidimensional Exploratory Displays (MEDs™)

Definitions Matter

Does agreeing to definitions for different types of data displays really matter? Yes, it matters a lot. You would never go to an architect and request plans for a teepee if what you really want is a wood-frame house. Why, then, is the same logic not applied to the creation of dashboards, reports, and multidimensional exploratory displays (MEDs™)?

Universally accepted and agreed-upon definitions are not superfluous. They are necessary (critical) to provide a framework and structure for users to understand what they are requesting, and for teams to know what they should be creating. Definitions are required to create a plan and a path forward for creating data displays in alignment with what people need to make informed decisions, and when appropriate, drive action. The Cheshire Cat in Lewis Carroll's *Alice in Wonderland* may have said it best when Alice asks: "Would you tell me, please, which way I ought to go from here?" to which the Cat responds: "If you don't know where you are going, any road will take you there."

Definitions are the clear starting place, but how to successfully design these types of displays is also critical. Therefore, each section of this chapter explains the purpose/objection of each display type; the level of data to be displayed (i.e., summaries vs. details); and design guidelines and tips.

Dashboards

The use of the term *dashboard* when referring to data displays is so ubiquitous that it may very well be destined to land in the dustbin of semantic satiation. "Semantic satiation" is not an attempt at humor, it is an actual term coined from extensive research that describes a word that has been repeated so many times, and with loose interpretations, that it becomes meaningless.

Dashboards Defined

A car dashboard provides a familiar example of the distinguishing characteristics of information dashboards and a foundation upon which to create a definition (Figure 10.1).

Purpose/Objective

The goal of a car dashboard is to display essential monitoring information required to help a person safely drive from Point A to Point B.

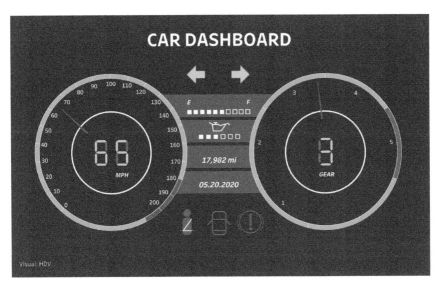

FIGURE 10.1   Car dashboard example.

Data/Information

The dashboard displays a summary of key metrics that provide situational awareness in support of the driver's objective. Metrics such as:

- Fuel level
- Doors or trunk ajar
- Speed
- Seatbelts buckled
- Engine warning lights

The dashboard is a single visual display that may be monitored at-a-glance. It requires no or few interactions such as indicator selection by the driver to display key metrics, and it is continuously updated as the underlying data changes. It also leverages preattentive attributes with things like blinking lights to grab the driver's attention about important information.

Now compare these characteristics to data visualization expert Stephen Few's definition of an information dashboard (Few, 2013, 26).

> ## A dashboard is a visual display
>
> of
> ## The most important information needed to achieve one or more objectives
> that has been
> ## consolidated on a single computer screen
> so it can be
> ## monitored at a glance.

More recently, Few offered an updated definition that he uses in combination with the original to provide additional clarity:

> ## A dashboard is a predominantly visual information display that people use to rapidly monitor current conditions that require a timely response to fulfill a specific role.

Few's definition(s) succinctly explain an information dashboard, and when referred to frequently provide the touchstone required to design beautiful and useful dashboards.

Design

The requirements for designing beautiful dashboards that people love to use are discussed throughout this book. They include:

- Selecting the metrics to be displayed in alignment with a user's scope, role/responsibilities, and decisions they need to make
- Leveraging people's visual capabilities
- Fidelity to the best practices of table and chart design
- Providing meaningful context for metrics: "compared to what"
- Leveraging Gestalt Principles by organizing information in a logical arrangement to support correct comparisons while being careful not to signal incorrect or meaningless comparisons
- Creating clear labels and intuitive navigation

- Not exceeding the boundaries of one screen
- Few or no data selection or filter requirements by the user to render the needed display of data
- Supporting further inquiry through focused reports, detailed lists and tables, and exploratory tools through Guided Analytics (see Figure 3.2)

Example Dashboards

Hospital Chief Executive Officer Dashboard

This dashboard (Figure 10.2) was designed to address the scope, role, decisions and current environment in which a hospital chief executive officer (CEO) has to navigate—an environment shaped

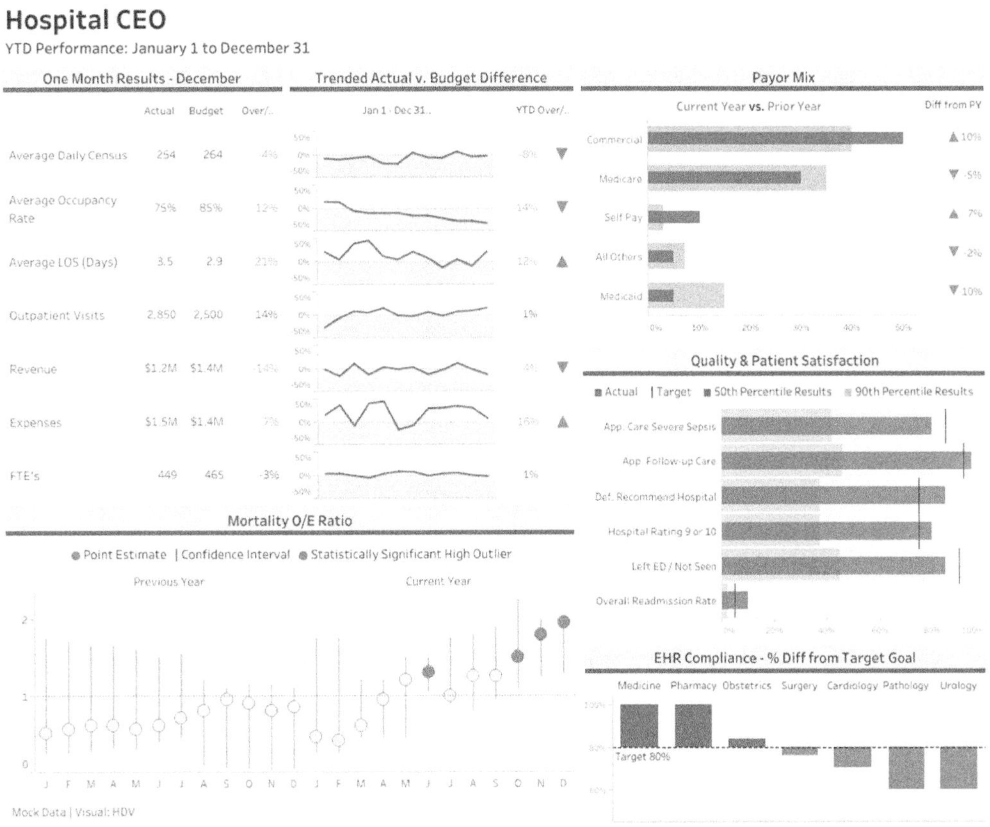

FIGURE 10.2 Hospital CEO dashboard example.

by value-based purchasing (VBP) and public reporting, where financial, clinical, information technology, and patient satisfaction results are all inextricably linked. The concept of VBP and the underlying driver of the information that hospital CEOs require to be successful is that healthcare purchasers (payors, patients) should hold healthcare providers (hospitals, doctors, etc.) accountable for both the cost and quality of care they deliver.

In the "One Month Results" section of the dashboard are industry-standard metrics about the hospital's occupancy rate and average daily census along with high-level results—revenue and expenses—all compared to budget. Up and down icons are used to alert the CEO to specific areas that may require further inquiry, along with sparkline deviation graphs that feature direct variances of actual performance compared to the budget for the past 12 months.

The "Payor Mix" section allows the CEO to easily monitor any changes to the payor mix from the previous year to the current year. This is information that helps to inform many of the financial management decisions made by a hospital, and makes it easy to see any significant changes.

The "Quality and Patient Satisfaction" sections display composite results for categories of mandated performance measures using a bullet graph. This hospital's results—the teal bars—are compared to internal targets that have been set for each measure—represented by the vertical black lines. Three comparative national results are displayed with a bar in the background that uses different gradients of the color gray to show different percentile results. As is evident in this display, bullet graphs are especially useful to display lots of comparative data in a limited space. (Note, keys must always be included close to this type of display so the viewer can understand the different comparative color values being displayed.) Displaying the information in this manner allows a CEO to understand how well the staff is performing and where they may need to improve.

Substantial financial investments, and the promise of improved patient care, meant that hospital CEOs were also carefully monitoring EHR compliance. The deviation bar chart makes it possible for a CEO to easily and quickly see which departments are and are not meeting their targets and where attention should be focused.

Hospital CEOs cannot afford any surprises about their overall and specific performance, especially on metrics such as observed versus expected mortality ratios (O/E). On this dashboard, a point is used to display each month's O/E mortality point estimate, and a line shows the confidence intervals. If the O/E is statistically significant for a particular month, the color orange is used to ensure the viewer sees it. Like the bullet graphs, a key is placed directly near the display in order that the user can interpret the display.

Syndromic Surveillance Dashboard

This example dashboard (Figure 10.3) was designed to help public health department leaders and managers who are responsible for monitoring syndromic surveillance data, and protecting the public health of communities. Using publicly available data from the NYC Department of Health and Mental Hygiene (DoHMH) captured at the beginning of the COVID-19 (coronavirus disease of 2019) pandemic presented a unique opportunity to demonstrate the power of a simple, easy to understand and use dashboard that allows people to rapidly monitor critical public health data.

Designed as an electronic, interactive dashboard that is continuously updated as data and information come into the department, this dashboard displays a table of summary data by syndromic categories (i.e., diseases or sets of symptoms) such as asthma, diarrhea, influenza-like diseases, respiratory, and vomiting. The labels for these categories are blue and underlined signaling to viewers that if they click on them an action will occur.

In this dashboard all of the graphs will change to show data and information about that specific syndrome (influenza-like Illness is selected in this example). The values in the table are by week and show the count of reported cases for the current selected timeframe, the average for years prior, and the percent change. A small

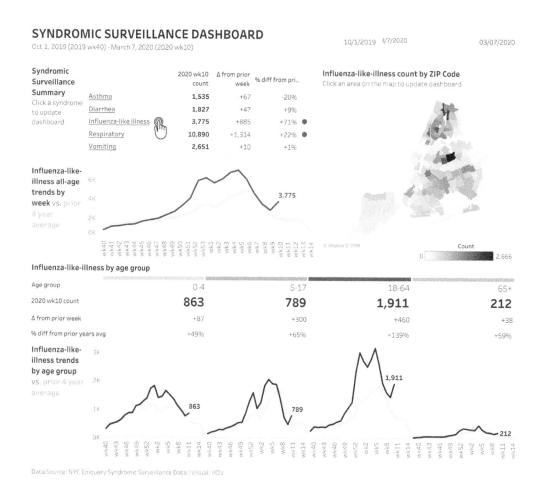

FIGURE 10.3   Public health syndromic surveillance dashboard.

dot icon on the table of different saturations of the color red (the saturations indicate the intensity of the percent change) is designed to leverage preattentive attributes—to signal to the viewer "Look here, there is something important you need to see." The line graph in the top half of the dashboard shows all reported cases over the weeks selected. The line graphs on the bottom of the dashboard are stratified by age groups. An interactive map shows the count of cases by ZIP codes and each area on the map may be selected by the viewer, thereby changing the dashboard to display information just for that area. This enables public health professionals to monitor and investigate trends that may be out of the norm and alarming.

DASHBOARD DESIGN TIPS:

- Dashboards are not comprehensive. Therefore, adopt and use a Guided Analytics Framework (see Figure 3.2) to create supporting reports, lists, and exploratory tools that provide the required contextual information about critical metrics being displayed on a dashboard.

- Research the available data and any taxonomies and categories they may be part of and that will make them easy to summarize on a dashboard (see Chapter 2).

- Research and understand the user's scope, role/responsibilities, and the decisions they need to make, and the organizational hierarchy in which they work. For example, if a manager is responsible for ten clinics' financial performance, consider a dashboard that displays a few key financial metrics for all ten of them. This helps managers to understand at-a-glance which clinic may need the most attention. Then create a dashboard that displays a more significant number of metrics for each clinic and provides additional context about that clinic's specific performance (see Chapter 3).

- Limit the number of selections and filters that users have to make to see key metrics quickly and easily, at-a-glance (remember the car dashboard example). One tip to reduce selection overload is to ask: "Can this indicator be displayed on the dashboard?" For example, instead of creating a payor type or a medical condition filter, determine if the information can be summarized and displayed directly on the dashboard. Remember, more information and details may be easily accessed if dashboards are part of a logical framework.

Dashboard Summary

Figuring out how to adequately summarize oceans of health and healthcare data in a meaningful and usable way on a dashboard can be challenging, but it is achievable. Start with a working definition, adopt design methods, practice, and test. Through collaborative trial and error and a commitment to always improving, the process will become less intimidating and the resulting dashboards will be more beautiful and usable.

Reports

As is true for an information dashboard, having a working definition for a report is necessary to ensure that data visualization designers and the teams they collaborate with, know and agree about what it is they are creating.

Reports Defined

Whereas a dashboard is a display of summary data and information created for the purpose of monitoring current conditions, a report is a comprehensive, descriptive, and detailed account of data and information about those conditions or other topics, occurrences, or issues that require a more thorough examination.

Purpose/Objective

The purpose of a report is to deliver in-depth contextual information viewers need to understand different conditions, topics, occurrences, or issues in order that they may gain deeper insights and make informed decisions.

Design

Reports may be static or electronic.

- Static reports are almost always handcrafted each time they are created or updated.
- They usually include a written narrative of one or more pages, and some charts and graphs to illustrate key points.
- They are published either in a paper format, or through a document or PDF that may be accessed electronically.

- Updates and modifications to them are almost always manual.
- Reports may also be preformatted designs that are electronic, interactive, one screen or longer (i.e., require scrolling), and include some limited selection filters (e.g., region, department, medical condition) and other interactivity such as linking to other reports or resources.
- They are predominantly comprised of charts and graphs, and may also include some short narratives, which may also be dynamic.
- Electronic reports may be updated on a continuous basis (minute by minute, weekly, monthly, quarterly, annually, etc.) from an underlying dynamic database, or manually updated, for example, with new data uploads on either a regular or ad-hoc basis.

Example Reports

Foundation Annual Report (Static)

The inclusion of select graphs in static reports of all types can serve to highlight important information the author needs to impart to the reader. The type of graph can range from a scatterplot to display study results in a scientific research paper, to a bar chart or line graph (or some other appropriate type) highlighting important issues in a group's annual report. No matter what the report is about, the data to be displayed using a graph must deliver important insights and engage the reader in a meaningful way.

The following examples (Figure 10.4) are from the grant-making Donaghue Foundation Annual Report. Select projects the Foundation has provided financial support to are highlighted and include information about:

- Grantee's name, credentials/title, affiliation, and research project name
- Contribution this project will have to improving the value of patient care
- Goal of the project and the problem it will study
- Approach of the researcher and how the results will be translated from the bench to the bedside

Greater Value Portfolio Research Spotlight

IMPACT OF A MULTIFACETED EARLY MOBILITY INTERVENTION ON
OUTCOMES AND ICU-ACQUIRED MORBIDITIES IN CRITICALLY ILL CHILDREN

Sapna R. Kudchakar, MD, PhD, Johns Hopkins University

Contribution to Improved Value

Value refers to both how much we pay and, just as importantly, the outcomes we get for that cost

About this project

The goal of this project is to determine the impact of an early mobility program on children in ICUs and assess facilitators and barriers to its wider implementation. The two-year award is for $443,448. The partnering organizations are four tertiary-care pediatric ICUs of diverse size, setting, and geographic location.

The Problem

Although mortality in pediatric ICUs has decreased, long-term ICU stays are associated with longer immobility, heavier sedation, and insufficient delirium prevention that increase ICU-acquired morbidities and hospital lengths of stays.

Project Approach

A pilot study of a multi-intervention program to promote early mobility, efficient sleep, and delirium prevention had positive results for safety and feasibility. This study will assess patient-level clinical outcomes and will indentify facilitators and barriers to facility-level success in implementing the program.

Translating Research into Practice

In addition to traditional scholarly dissemination, translation approaches include developing key messages for stakeholders and researchers from the partnering organizations, summaries in lay language about the benefits of an early mobility program for families, and a set of summaries, tools and resources for clinicians.

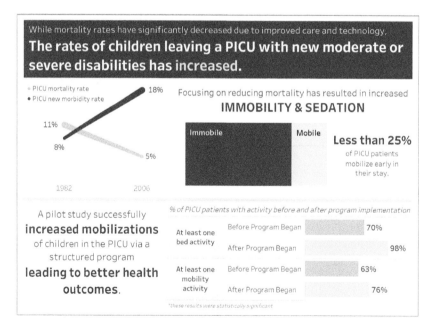

FIGURE 10.4   Donaghue Foundation static report example.

Source: Donaghue Foundation

In the first example (Figure 10.4) a slopegraph is used to display the problem "Children leaving the Pediatric Intensive Care Unit (PICU) with disabilities has significantly increased from 1982 to 2006." A stacked bar chart displays how the focus on reducing child mortality has resulted in their increased immobility and sedation. Horizontal bar charts show the results of a pilot project to increase these children's mobility activities in an effort to reduce disabilities after a PICU stay, and which are the proposed activities to be supported and studied by this grantee. All of the key data points about this research project have been displayed using simple graphs and clear labels. And, because this is included as part of the annual report, colors and layout have been selected to reflect the Foundation's overall branding.

When including graphs in a static report it is paramount to select the data and information that will encapsulate the important points of the report. The addition of graphs for no reason other than to make a report more "attractive" will only add distracting clutter.

Hospital Readmission Population Comparison Report (Dynamic, Interactive)

The following example (Figure 10.5) is an electronic, interactive, preformatted report focused on one specific outcome—readmission to the hospital within 30 days of discharge. It is designed and formatted to compare patients who were readmitted versus those who were not readmitted in order that hospital teams may gain insights into any potential differences in the two cohorts that may help them to change care processes or clinical protocols.

The design includes a few selection filters across the top: hospital, department, service, discharge date. This allows users to make selections and see the data in the report displayed through the departments of interest to them, for example, orthopedic versus medicine departments. Additional refinement of the data being displayed may be accomplished by clicking on specific conditions of interest (based on analysis and public reporting requirements of the Centers for Medicare and Medicaid (CMS) of conditions most

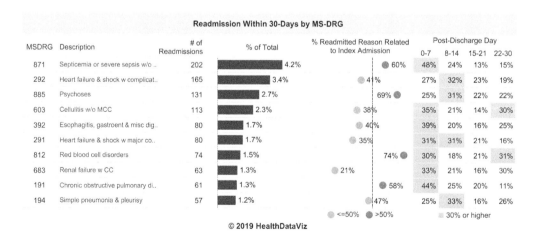

Hospital Readmission Population Comparison

Hospital: All, Department: All, Service: Family Medicine, Reporting Period: 8/7/2017 to 8/8/2017

HealthDataViz   DATA DEFINITIONS   INFO

Hospital	Department	Service	Discharge Date	1/1/2016 to 8/31/2018
Hospital 2	All	Family Medicine	All	

Overall Readmission within 30 Days

Of the **42,894** cases between discharged between January 1, 2018 and August 31 2018, **14.0%** (n=5,884) were readmitted.

Among those readmitted, **49.0%** (n=2,883) were for the same condition and **51.0%** (n=3,001) were for a different condition.

284 unique MS-DRGs had readmissions.

Readmissions by Index Admission Condition

Click a condition below to filter results

AMI	CABG	COPD	HF	PN	THA/ SKA
6%	12%	14%	18%	21%	9%

Patient Profile

		Readmitted	Not Readmitted	Difference (● higher for readmitted)
Gender	Female	43%	51%	-8%
	Male	57%	49%	8% ●
Age	19-44	19%	29%	-10%
	45-64	38%	31%	7% ●
	65+	44%	39%	5% ●
Length of Stay (LOS)	LOS Expected	6.5	6.7	-0.2
	LOS Observed	6.6	5.9	0.7 ●

View more by: Payor   (Top 10 only)

	Readmitted	Not Readmitted	Difference
Medicare Traditional	44%	31%	13% ●
Medicaid Traditional	13%	14%	-1%
Other	13%	11%	2% ●
Medicare/Managed Care	11%	12%	-1%
Medicaid/Managed Care	10%	12%	-2%
Commercial/Private	9%	20%	-11%

Readmission Within 30-Days by MS-DRG

MSDRG	Description	# of Readmissions	% of Total	% Readmitted Reason Related to Index Admission	Post-Discharge Day 0-7	8-14	15-21	22-30
871	Septicemia or severe sepsis w/o ..	202	4.2%	● 60%	48%	24%	13%	15%
292	Heart failure & shock w complicat..	165	3.4%	● 41%	27%	32%	23%	19%
885	Psychoses	131	2.7%	69% ●	25%	31%	22%	22%
603	Cellulitis w/o MCC	113	2.3%	● 38%	35%	21%	14%	30%
392	Esophagitis, gastroent & misc dig..	80	1.7%	● 40%	39%	20%	16%	25%
291	Heart failure & shock w major co..	80	1.7%	● 35%	31%	31%	21%	16%
812	Red blood cell disorders	74	1.5%	74% ●	30%	18%	21%	31%
683	Renal failure w CC	63	1.3%	● 21%	33%	21%	16%	30%
191	Chronic obstructive pulmonary di..	61	1.3%	● 58%	44%	25%	20%	11%
194	Simple pneumonia & pleurisy	57	1.2%	● 47%	25%	33%	16%	26%

● <=50%   ● >50%   ▓ 30% or higher

© 2019 HealthDataViz

FIGURE 10.5   Readmission event vs. no event comparison report.

frequently having a readmission) and displayed in the bar chart in the upper right of the report. Using the color blue with an underline is a visual cue that most viewers are familiar with, they know when they click on it an action will occur. In this report, all of the data on the report changes to display just the information related to the condition selected. There is a short summary narrative in the upper left that dynamically updates the metrics based on the user's selection.

The first set of horizontal bar charts display the two cohorts of patients, (i.e., those who were vs. those who were not readmitted). On the next set of horizontal bars located in the middle left-hand side of the report additional selection options are provided which allow the viewer to change the bar charts below it to display more about each cohort such as payor, discharge status, or admission source. Orange points are used to grab attention to differences that are higher in the readmitted cohort.

At the bottom of the report, detailed information about the MS-DRGs that were observed for the readmitted patients is displayed. Anchoring this section in the MS-DRG description labels and orienting the bars horizontally leverages the fact that people viewing this report read from left to right, and makes it possible to pack a lot of contextual data on each row, such as the patient count, percent of total, percent of patients' readmission that was related to their index admission reason, and the distribution of post-discharge days after which the readmission occurred.

This report is designed to provide additional and extensive contextual information about the patients being readmitted and help providers make informed decisions about where they might focus their efforts to reduce readmissions. And, although this example is designed as an interactive, electronic report, all of the graphs and charts are suitable for inclusion in a static report.

REPORT DESIGN TIPS:

- Go back to basics. When creating a report focused on a specific issue or topic, create an outline and format to help guide the different report sections to ensure the information and data are clear and impactful.

- Include as much contextual information and data as is necessary to fully understand and consider a condition, topic, or issue. This may include data such as dates and times, locations, specific characteristics about a population, or other contributing factors that may have an impact on the results being observed. Remember, in data analysis and reporting the only way to gain valuable insights is to provide meaningful context, to answer the questions "compared with what?" and "so what?"

- Dynamic, electronic reports provide the advantage of allowing the viewer to select filters and change the views, but they must not be overly burdensome. Determine what data need to be included on a report and then create selection filters to display them through different prisms, such as those shown in Figure 10.5.

Report Summary

Understanding the fundamental difference between a report and a dashboard will significantly reduce confusion and frustration about what is to be designed and created. Establishing a process and using a structure, such as the Guided Analytics Framework described in Chapter 3, will also help teams to map out what data, at what level of detail, should be displayed in a dashboard versus a report.

Multidimensional Exploratory Displays (MEDs™)

Multidimensional Exploratory Displays MEDs™ are data displays that allow a user to go on an exploratory journey or fact-finding mission. (A search was undertaken for a name that best described this type of display, but nothing we found resonated with us.

Therefore, we created our own name, and given our focus on health and healthcare it was the acronym MEDs™ that sealed the deal.)

MEDs™ Defined

MEDs™ are electronic query tools that display different facts about a dataset using graphs, tables, and some limited narrative, based almost entirely on the user's inputs and selections.

Purpose/Objective

The purpose of MEDs™ is to support freestyle queries and an ad-hoc approach to exploring datasets. The determination about what data to view is entirely in the hands of the user, and powered by their imagination and curiosity about what the data might reveal.

Design

Extensive user-defined data querying functionality is core to MEDs™. Advanced MEDs™ may also provide additional selection criteria, which allows the end user to decide what type of graph will be used to display query results, such as a bar, line, map, or table.

As the name conveys, Multidimensional Exploratory Displays are fundamentally different than dashboards and reports, which are carefully designed to provide data and insights in alignment with a particular role or focused topic, and which provide only limited, predetermined data selection and filtering capability.

Example MED™

New York City Department of Health and Mental Hygiene | EpiQuery

An example of this type of data query and display tool is the New York City Department of Health and Mental Hygiene (DoHMH) EpiQuery system. A contraction of the words *epidemiology* and *query*, the objective of this MED™ is to reduce the barriers and encourage users, from novice to advanced, to explore, probe, and question the extensive public health survey and surveillance data captured by the DoHMH.

In the following example (Figure 10.6), the first display shows the available data arranged by survey instrument or topic. A heat map table displays the indicator name, the years, and volume of data available for each one. The design is purposely simple to ensure novice users who may not have any knowledge or experience with the Department's data will find it easy to explore.

The data being displayed may be changed using selection choices displayed directly on the page, and each box on the heat map may be clicked to navigate to an overview about that indicator. Rather than having to navigate in and out of the displays to select new surveys, indicators, or years, the user can make those selections directly on the page they are viewing. As new selections are made, the information is passed to all pages and displays, thereby eliminating the need to repeatedly make the same selections on different views of the data. Users may also jump between pages by clicking on the blue navigation bars at the top of each page.

After extensive research, persona development, and other methods described in Chapter 3, it was determined that these different pages should build one upon the next, with each page becoming increasingly complex. (Note: These pages do not need to be accessed sequentially by an experienced user, but they are arranged in that way for the reasons given.) In addition to increasingly complex capabilities to analyze the data, the user may choose different, appropriate charts and graphs, such as bars, lines, maps and tables, to view the data.

An example and explanation about one type of functionality of these MEDs™ is shown and described in Figures 10.7, 10.8, and 10.9, which imagines that a user is interested in exploring data about NYC residents' smoking habits.

The indicator named Smoking Status, Never Smoked (captured in the Community Health Survey) for 2017 was selected and then the Analyze by Neighborhood tab at the top (in dark blue) was selected. The top half of the display shows the age-adjusted estimate of the prevalence of NYC residents who responded they had never smoked, currently smoke, or were former smokers in the horizontal bar chart. Because the original selection was "Never Smoked" the maps and graphs are displaying the values for that indicator response and are labeled as such. The labels on the bar chart are blue and underlined, thereby signaling to the user that if they click on them something will occur—in this example, all of the displays will change to show the values associated with the indicator responses (Never, Current, Former). A line graph at the bottom of the display shows the trend over all of the results from 2002 to 2017.

Selections located on the top right allow the user to make different choices of an indicator, year, and whether or not to show adjusted or non-adjusted age estimated data. The graph type may also be changed from a map to a bar or table of the results as shown in Figures 10.8 and 10.9. In these views, specific regions may be selected (blue-underlined region labels on bars and table) to view their prevalence and trends.

The name EpiQuery provides a clear description about what the application is designed to do—query (question, probe, look into) epidemiology data—as well as a perfect example of a Multidimensional Exploratory Display.

MEDs™ DESIGN TIPS:

- Historically MEDs™ have been designed for use by experts. However, in the expanding environment of publicly available health and healthcare data, new designs must reduce barriers for novice users.
- Apply careful guardrails such as suppression of small sample sizes and clear messaging about statistical significance of results to try to ensure the responsible interpretation and use of the data.
- All data and tool documentation must be clearly visible, easy to access, and written in plain language.
- Only allow data to be displayed using the correct graph type, and format the results in keeping with the best practices of data visualization.

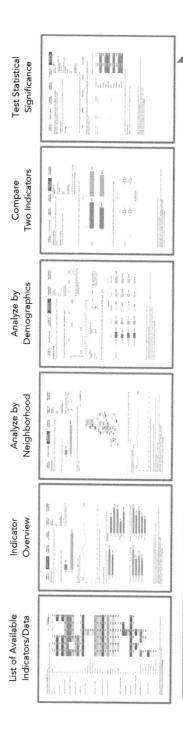

List of Available Indicators/Data   Indicator Overview   Analyze by Neighborhood   Analyze by Demographics   Compare Two Indicators   Test Statistical Significance

Simple overviews for novice users to increasingly more complex views and interactivity for advanced users.

Data Source: NYC DoHMH Epiquery https://a816-health.nyc/gov/hdi/epiquery I Visual: HDV

FIGURE 10.6 Exploratory functionality and views designed for a wide range of users and skills.

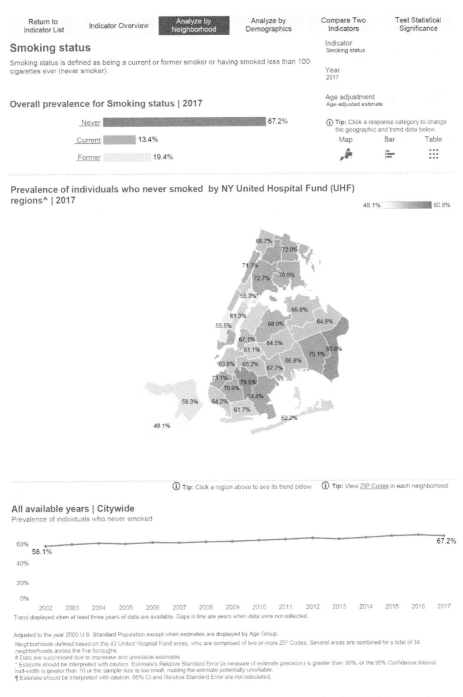

FIGURE 10.7 Prevalence of individuals who never smoked (2017) by neighborhood/map.

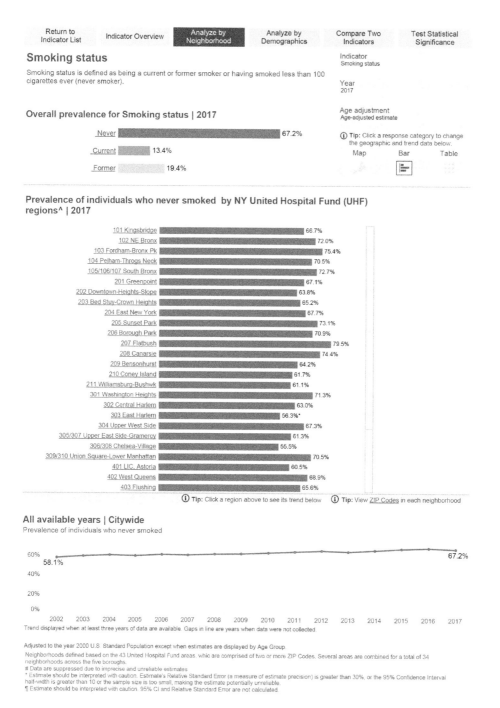

FIGURE 10.8   Prevalence of individuals who never smoked (2017) by neighborhood/bars.

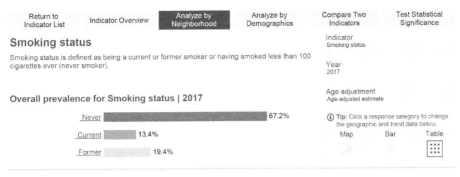

| Return to Indicator List | Indicator Overview | Analyze by Neighborhood | Analyze by Demographics | Compare Two Indicators | Test Statistical Significance |

Smoking status

Smoking status is defined as being a current or former smoker or having smoked less than 100 cigarettes ever (never smoker).

indicator
Smoking status

Year
2017

Age adjustment
Age-adjusted estimate

Overall prevalence for Smoking status | 2017

Never		67.2%
Current		13.4%
Former		19.4%

(i) **Tip:** Click a response category to change the geographic and trend data below.

Map   Bar   Table

Prevalence of individuals who never smoked by NY United Hospital Fund (UHF) regions^ | 2017

	Prevalence	Lower Confidence Interval	Upper Confidence Interval	Population
101 Kingsbridge	66.7%	56.3%	75.7%	48,000
102 NE Bronx	72.0%	63.8%	79.0%	104,000
103 Fordham-Bronx Pk	75.4%	69.4%	80.6%	144,000
104 Pelham-Throgs Neck	70.5%	63.7%	76.6%	166,000
105/106/107 South Bronx	72.7%	68.1%	76.8%	296,000
201 Greenpoint	67.1%	56.9%	75.8%	69,000
202 Downtown-Heights-Slope	63.8%	57.4%	69.8%	117,000
203 Bed Stuy-Crown Heights	65.2%	59.5%	70.6%	164,000
204 East New York	67.7%	60.1%	74.5%	94,000
205 Sunset Park	73.1%	65.5%	79.6%	73,000
206 Borough Park	70.9%	64.6%	76.5%	174,000
207 Flatbush	79.5%	74.2%	84.0%	187,000
208 Canarsie	74.4%	66.6%	81.0%	116,000
209 Bensonhurst	64.2%	55.7%	71.9%	106,000
210 Coney Island	61.7%	54.7%	68.2%	148,000
211 Williamsburg-Bushwk	61.1%	53.5%	68.3%	104,000
301 Washington Heights	71.3%	64.0%	77.6%	148,000
302 Central Harlem	63.0%	54.2%	70.9%	78,000
303 East Harlem	56.3%*	44.3%*	67.6%*	47,000*
304 Upper West Side	67.3%	57.8%	75.5%	123,000
305/307 Upper East Side-Gramercy	61.3%	54.2%	68.0%	189,000
306/308 Chelsea-Village	55.5%	47.0%	63.7%	118,000
309/310 Union Square-Lower Manhattan	70.5%	62.2%	77.7%	152,000

(i) **Tip:** Click a region above to see its trend below   (i) **Tip:** View ZIP Codes in each neighborhood

All available years | Citywide
Prevalence of individuals who never smoked

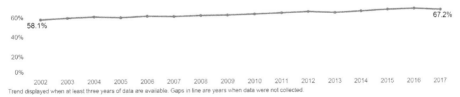

Trend displayed when at least three years of data are available. Gaps in line are years when data were not collected.

Adjusted to the year 2000 U.S. Standard Population except when estimates are displayed by Age Group.

Neighborhoods defined based on the 43 United Hospital Fund areas, which are comprised of two or more ZIP Codes. Several areas are combined for a total of 34 neighborhoods across the five boroughs.
\# Data are suppressed due to imprecise and unreliable estimates
* Estimate should be interpreted with caution. Estimate's Relative Standard Error (a measure of estimate precision) is greater than 30%, or the 95% Confidence Interval half-width is greater than 10 or the sample size is too small, making the estimate potentially unreliable.
¶ Estimate should be interpreted with caution. 95% CI and Relative Standard Error are not calculated.

FIGURE 10.9   Prevalence of individuals who never smoked (2017) by neighborhood/table.

MEDs™ Summary

Far too often the types of MEDs™ described here are called dashboards. They are not. Each type of display, dashboards, reports, MEDs™, has a unique set of characteristics and purpose, and failing to understand this results in displays that are neither satisfying nor useful.

Summary

The types of dashboards, reports, and MEDs™ described here are often an integral part of the Guided Analytics Framework described in Chapter 3. Using this type of framework and other techniques described in the chapter, along with definitions of what is to be designed, is extraordinarily helpful in ensuring the right views and tools are being designed for the right personas and use cases.

Quite simply, great care must be taken to display the right data in the right way for the right audience.

Chapter Eleven

Infographics

The term *infographic* is a combination of the words "information" and "graphic." As a visual representation of information, data, and knowledge, infographics have two important attributes which help to define them—they are topical, and crafted to achieve an intended outcome—such as raising viewers' awareness of a subject or issue, teaching them something new, persuading them of a specific point of view, or moving them to take action.

The information dashboards, described in Chapter 10, deliver continually (i.e., on a regular schedule) updated data in the form of key metrics selected to help monitor performance and manage workplaces and conditions. Infographics, in contrast, are crafted using carefully researched data and information from reliable, recognized, and trusted sources that support the designer's intended message. As Martino notes, "usually there are several stories in the data—you have to select one. You can change the visualization by putting emphasis on a different story" (Offenhuber, 2010).

Infographics have been used most frequently in journalism (newspapers and magazines, both print and electronic) to make complicated issues and information more engaging and understandable. This makes for another distinguishing characteristic of infographics—they are usually one-and-done pieces published with the data and information available at the time they were created. Depending on the publishing medium and technology used to create them, infographics may be static or interactive.

More recently, infographics have grown in popularity across numerous sectors, including health and healthcare, as people's interest in reading long-form narratives has waned and advances in technology have made them easy to create and disseminate. Infographics that hit their mark are engaging, visually pleasing, sometimes fun, and always informative compositions of well-crafted narratives, data visualizations, graphic design, and typography.

"No Tobacco Day" Infographic

To Raise Awareness, Teach, Persuade. An infographic is an excellent visual display choice for quickly raising awareness, teaching, and sometimes even persuading a viewer to a specific point of view about a topic. The infographic, "Ending Smoking Around the World" (Figure 11.1), was created in recognition of the World Health Organization's "No Tobacco Day." Using data from 2000–2008 as the baseline, and comparing it to the same data captured from 2014–2017, this infographic raises awareness about the percentage of cigarette smokers in different countries and the steps that specific countries have taken to reduce smoking. The use of the color black for the background gives a serious and foreboding feel to the piece, and provides a strong contrast that effectively promotes the infographic's elements, from the cigarette smoke and the bar chart that resembles cigarettes, to the text and other graphics. These elements are used to engage the viewer as the topic and information being displayed require a bit of study and focus by the viewer to be fully comprehended.

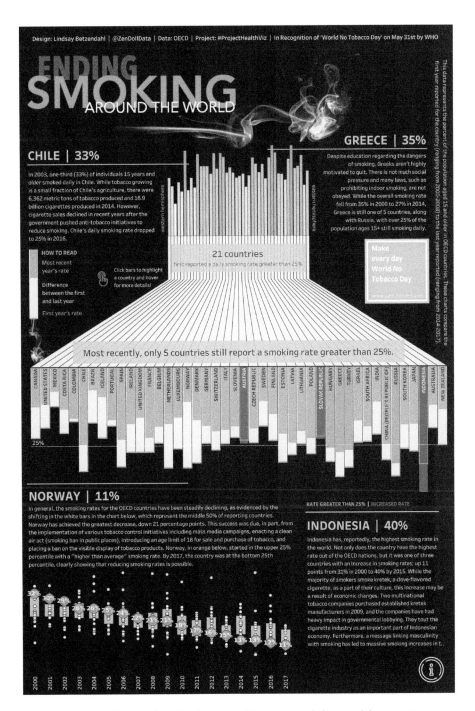

FIGURE 11.1 Infographic: Ending smoking around the world—to raise awareness, teach, persuade.

Source: Lindsay Betzendahl

Measles and Vaccinations Infographic

A Call to Action. The infographic "Measles" (Figure 11.2) is about the disease and a call to action to get vaccinated. This infographic tells a specific story, which is broken down into four visual sections, indicated by the vertical blue header on the left and horizontal separating lines; it is oriented to be read from top to bottom. The first section, "HISTORY," delivers a history of the disease; the next section, "OUTBREAKS," focuses on the resurgence of the disease and outbreaks in the United States; this is followed by the "GLOBAL IMPACT" section with displays about measles' impact worldwide; the last section, "GET VACCINATED," is a call to action for people to get vaccinated, and includes information about when the vaccine should be administered and who may not be a good candidate for it.

As explained in Chapter 4, visual images are much more likely to remain in our long-term memory than are numbers or text, and therefore play an important role in infographic design. Figure 11.2 has a number of illustrations to help convey complicated information in a memorable way: the graphic of the measles virus, the immunization calendar schedule, and the herd immunity rate graphic composed of people icons. The "GLOBAL IMPACT" may be viewed as a static graphic or online, where viewers can interact with the display to see more specific data by country. The choice of colors is consistent throughout the infographic and references those often found in health and healthcare: green for an illness or infection, blue for hospitals and other healthcare providers.

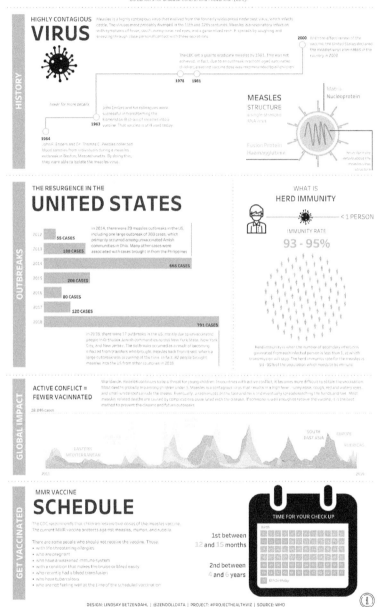

FIGURE 11.2 Infographic: Measles—A call to action.

TIPS FOR CREATING INFOGRAPHICS:

Graphic organizers. As described in Chapter 3, graphic organizers are invaluable tools in the development of any data display, including infographics. The use of graphic organizers helps to establish a hierarchy in the planning stage, identify the main components of the story, and define how those components will be sequenced on the page or screen (Cairo, 2013, 213). Before ever moving to development, designers can use these organizers to consider the critical questions, "What's the point?" and "What's the story?" (Cairo 2013, 216).

Outcome. Define the desired outcome of the display. Is it to raise awareness? teach? persuade? move to action?

Problem/Story. Define the problem or name the story to be showcased. Write a statement about the problem or theme of the story to refer to and use as a touchstone as the piece is developed.

Data and Information. Write a statement about why the problem being communicated is important and the point of story to be presented. Research data and statistics that are rigorous, truthful, and appropriate to support the problem and story. Research credible sources and reference materials to support the written narrative as well.

Summary/Call to Action. Summarize the problem and point of the piece. Call viewers to take action. Make clear what they can do and how to do it.

An infographic organizer approach need not follow this exact model and content, but will always provide a guide through an infographic in an orderly, logical manner, like a journalistic article or essay.

Infographic vs. Infoposter

As discussed in Chapter 10, the terms that we use to describe what we are creating matter. We can't call everything a dashboard and expect that designers, customers, and clients will all work in unison toward the same result if they all have a different vision of what is being created. The same is true with infographics. Is a true infographic being created, or is it really what design and visualization expert Connie Malamed referred to in her "Understanding Graphics" blog as an "infoposter"? The key difference is in the information being displayed and the intent of the piece. Merriam-Webster defines a "poster" as "a usually large printed sheet that often contains pictures and is posted in public (so as to promote something)." A poster is not the same as an infographic.

The following examples are classified as "infographics" on the publishing agencies' websites. However, they are really "infoposters." In Figure 11.3, "Stop the Spread of Germs," no information (i.e., data or statistics) is provided about infection rates or how the different recommendations reduce the spread of germs. Hence, there are no data visualization graphics. The message is focused solely on promoting ways to prevent the spread of respiratory diseases like COVID-19.

Figure 11.4, "Misusing and Overusing Antibiotics," is also categorized as an infographic on the publishing group's website, but it is actually an infoposter. Like the infoposter example in Figure 11.3, this example does not include any data or in-depth exploration about a topic; it is simply a poster to raise awareness of the risks of misusing and overusing antibiotics.

Stop the Spread of Germs

Help prevent the spread of respiratory diseases like COVID-19.

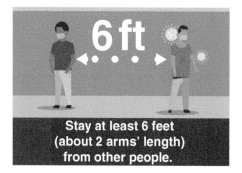

Stay at least 6 feet (about 2 arms' length) from other people.

Cover your cough or sneeze with a tissue, then throw the tissue in the trash and wash your hands.

When in public, wear a cloth face covering over your nose and mouth.

Do not touch your eyes, nose, and mouth.

Clean and disinfect frequently touched objects and surfaces.

Stay home when you are sick, except to get medical care.

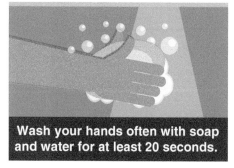

Wash your hands often with soap and water for at least 20 seconds.

cdc.gov/coronavirus

316917-A May 13, 2020 11:00 AM

FIGURE 11.3   Infoposter: Stop the spread of germs.

Misusing and overusing
ANTIBIOTICS
puts us all at risk

Taking antibiotics when they are not needed accelerates emergence of antibiotic resistance, **one of the biggest threats to global health**

You can help reduce antibiotic resistance

Overuse of antibiotics can cause bacteria to become resistant, meaning current treatments will no longer work

Always follow the advice of a qualified health care professional when taking antibiotics

Antibiotic resistant infections can lead to longer hospital stays, higher medical costs and more deaths

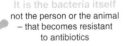

It is the bacteria itself not the person or the animal – that becomes resistant to antibiotics

Antibiotic resistant infections can **affect anyone,** of any age, in any country

When bacteria become resistant to antibiotics, common infections will no longer be treatable

World Health Organization

FIGURE 11.4   Infoposter: Misusing and overusing antibiotics.

Summary

Although the difference is not well described in the literature, it is important to differentiate between the more complex infographic and the infoposter. Understanding the difference will help to ensure that as teams collaborate, they clearly understand and agree on their objective.

Infoposters are far less complex than infographics, generally do not contain complex data, and are used to promote something, such as healthy behaviors. Well-designed infographics, whether static or interactive, include data about the topic and encourage study and exploration by viewers as they zoom in and analyze, measure, even manipulate the visual information in their minds. And though an infographic may be crafted to present a story with a specific point of view, it is the designer's responsibility to ensure that above all else, an infographic is accessible, engaging, and accurate.

Closing Thoughts and Recommended Reading and Resources

"I am still learning."

—*Michelangelo at age 87*

Closing Thoughts

Fluency and Mastery

Fluency and mastery at creating beautiful displays of data is not the result of natural talent. Rather, it is the result of an interest in the work, a willingness to practice, a sense of purpose, hope, and optimism.

These traits have been studied and written about by Angela Duckworth, most notably in her 2016 book, *Grit: The Power of Passion and Perseverance*. The central question she explores is "What is it that makes someone fluent, an expert or a master at something?" As Duckworth explains, "The thing that was revelatory to me was not that effort matters—everybody knows that effort matters. What was revelatory to me was how much it matters." She summarizes the characteristics and activities that are associated with a willingness and ability to stick with something and invest the effort in order to become a master expert as follows:

- *Interest*. Individuals who become experts or masters at something have an abiding interest and passion for it. They are interested and committed to the pursuit of learning and knowing more about it.
- *Deliberate Practice*. This concept is based on research by K. Anders Ericsson (2009), who found that experts do an intensive

kind of practice called "deliberate practice." Deliberative practices home in on weaknesses and self-assessment; it is practice that focuses on tasks beyond a person's current level of comfort and competence. Or in the words of Aristotle: "The roots of knowledge are bitter but the results are sweet." The fact that deliberate practice is hard means that the first characteristic, interest, is essential.

- *Sense of Purpose.* People at the top of their fields also describe their work as meaningful and having purpose. They are driven by helping others and doing or creating something that is beneficial to others.
- *Hope.* People who have achieved fluency and mastery also have hope. They're optimistic about the future and their ability to improve and effect change. They also believe that intelligence isn't fixed but can grow and change over time.

The results of this research are all supported by the author's individual and communal experiences. We are each interested in data visualization and we are always on the hunt for the latest idea, technique, and emerging research. We don't always love the feedback we hear, but we open the door wide to it because we know that without it, we live in an echo chamber of our own limited ideas and knowledge. We practice and struggle and fail, and fail again. But we just keep on trying until we figure it out, and hopefully get it right. We have a real sense of purpose—to improve the health of people and the delivery of healthcare through clear and compelling displays of data and information. And we are wildly optimistic and hopeful that the work matters and that all of our collective intelligence about a wide range of topics and issues can and will grow and change.

In closing and with a nod to our ongoing mastery and fluency journey, we welcome your inquiries and feedback and hope you have found this book helpful.

Bitten by the Viz Bug | Recommended Reading and Resources

Recommended Reading

Edward R. Tufte—Data viz devotees agree, he is our guru.

The Visual Display of Quantitative Information (1983). Cheshire, CT: Graphics Press.

Envisioning Information (1990). Cheshire, CT: Graphics Press.

Visual Explanations (1997). Cheshire, CT: Graphics Press.

Beautiful Evidence (2006). Cheshire, CT: Graphics Press.

Colin Ware—His books are on our lists of "must haves" for anyone who is truly serious about creating understandable and useful data visualizations. Ware's work is grounded in the research and scientific explanations about how our vision and cognition work, and how they inform the best practices of data visualization.

Information Visualization: Perception for Design (Interactive Technologies), 4th ed. (2020). Morgan Kaufman/Elsevier.

Alberto Cairo—A great thinker, chronicler, and challenger of the good, bad, and most importantly, the sometimes dangerously bad visualizations cluttering the universe.

The Functional Art: An Introduction to Information Graphics and Visualization (2013). New Riders.

The Truthful Art: Data, Charts, and Maps for Communication (2016). New Riders.

Bella Martin and Bruce Hanington—Experts in the methods of user-centered research, this team has written a really wonderful book with a simple, easy-to-use and follow layout that reflects their expertise.

Universal Methods of Design: 100 Ways to Research Complex Problems, Develop Innovative Ideas, and Design Effective Solutions (2012). Rockport Publishers.

Gretchen N. Peterson—Anyone who ever has to create a map should have a toolkit to refer to, and this book provides just that. Sections focus on color, typography, and composition patterns.

Cartographer's Toolkit: Colors, Typography, Patterns (2012). Peterson GIS.

Steve Krug—Krug's books are filled with great content and his keen wit makes this a fun read. These books are packed with testing and usability tips that are directly applicable to interactive data visualizations—a sorely overlooked part of the process when creating great data displays.

Rocket Surgery Made Easy: The Do-It-Yourself Guide to Finding and Fixing Usability Problems (2010). New Riders.

Don't Make Me Think, Revisited: A Common Sense Approach to Web Usability (2014). New Riders.

Alan Cooper—Widely recognized as the "Father of Visual Basic," Cooper pioneered the use of personas as practical interaction design tools to create high-tech products. Whenever asked what books folks should read to improve their knowledge and skills this one always makes the list—it is a classic.

The Inmates Are Running the Asylum: Why High-Tech Products Drive Us Crazy and How to Restore the Sanity (2004). Sam's Publishing.

Janice (Ginny) Redish—With a list of credentials and awards too long to list here, Ginny Redish's passion and expertise for creating products that work for the people who use them is evident throughout this book. Her principles and techniques extend beyond websites; they can and should be applied to any data display.

Letting Go of the Words: Writing Web Content that Works, 2nd ed. (2012). Morgan Kaufman/Elsevier.

Ellen Lupton—A preeminent design author and educator, and curator of contemporary design at Cooper-Hewitt, National Design Museum in New York, Lupton's book is an essential design tool, especially for anyone creating infographics.

Thinking with Type: A Critical Guide for Designers, Editors, & Students, 2nd ed. (2010). Princeton Architectural Press.

Resources

Cartographer's Toolkit by Gretchen Peterson, 2012

Designing Better Maps by Cynthia Brewer, 2015.

The Best Boring Book Ever of Tableau for Healthcare, 4th Edition by: Benevento, Steeger, Rowell, 2020. HDV Publisher available on Amazon.

When Maps Should Not Be Maps by Matthew Ericson, http://www.ericson.net/content/2011/10/when-maps-shouldnt-be-maps/

Accessibility Resources

- Section 508 Creating Accessible Digital Products: https://www.section508.gov/create
- WebAIM Designing for Screen Reader Compatibility: https://webaim.org/techniques/screenreader/
- Venngage Colorblind-Friendly Palettes: https://venngage.com/blog/colorblind-friendly-palette/
- Color Brewer: http://colorbrewer2.org
- WebAIM Contrast Checker: https://webaim.org/resources/contrastchecker/

Author Bios

Katherine Rowell, MS, MHA

 Kathy Rowell is a nationally recognized health, healthcare, and data visualization expert, lecturer, and author specializing in helping leading organizations analyze, design, and present visual displays of data to inform their decisions and stimulate effective action. She is the co-author of the Best Boring Book Ever (BBBE) of Healthcare Classification Systems and Databases, and BBBE of Tableau for Healthcare Professionals, which are used by numerous colleges and universities and professional organizations to teach and train students and professionals. Kathy is the Co-founder and Principal of HealthDataViz (HDV) where she has led innovative and ground-breaking projects and data visualization training initiatives for leading organizations such as Memorial Sloan Kettering Cancer Center, the Centers for Medicare and Medicaid Services, and the Children's Hospital Association. A graduate of the University of NH and Dartmouth Medical School, Kathy lives in Maine and loves being on the water and cruising the coast with her family on their boat "Visualize."

Kathy

Lindsay Betzendahl, MA, MFT

 With seven years wholly immersed in healthcare data visualization, following ten years as a licensed marriage and family therapist, Lindsay brings a wealth of direct care experience and an unbridled passion and nationally recognized expertise for visualizing health and healthcare data. A Tableau Zen Master and member of the HealthDataViz (HDV) team, Lindsay is an enthusiastic creator of effective, intuitive, and beautiful dashboards that people love to use and make the story and opportunities buried in the data clear. Her passion for health and healthcare data knows no bounds evidenced by her establishment of #ProjectHealthViz, a community of passionate data visualizers that create displays of health and healthcare data each month to tell our health stories. Lindsay has a B.A. from Bucknell University and an M.A. from the University of Connecticut. She currently lives in Pennsylvania with her husband and two boys.

Cambria Brown, MPH

Cambria Brown has over ten years of experience analyzing and visualizing health and healthcare data, and is a Tableau Desktop Certified Professional. With a background in public health, survey design, advanced biostatistics, and quality improvement, Cambria understands the full data use cycle and is passionate about helping organizations use data to improve health. As a member of the HealthDataViz team, she has developed beautiful, user-friendly, and high impact dashboards for a variety of clients including the New York City Dept. of Health and Mental Hygiene, the Colorado Dept. of Public Health and Environment, and the Urban Indian Health Institute. Cambria holds a Master of Public Health in Epidemiology and Biostatistics from Oregon Health & Science University. She lives in Colorado where, when not data vizzing, she enjoys going on adventures with her husband and two children.

References

Introduction

Wennberg, *The Dartmouth Atlas*, https://www.dartmouthatlas.org/downloads/reports/Cancer_report_11_16_10.pdf.

Chapter 3

Martin, Bella, and Bruce Hanington, 2012. *Universal Methods of Design: 100 Ways to Research Complex Problems, Develop Innovative Ideas, and Design Effective Solutions*. Rockport Publishers.

Chapter 4

Attention span research: http://dl.motamem.org/microsoft-attention-spans-research-report.pdf.

Soegaard, Mads, 2019. *The Power of White Space*. Interaction Design Foundation, https://www.interactiondesign.org/literature/article/the-power-of-white-space.

Ware, Colin, 2004, 2020. *Information Visualization: Perception for Design*. Morgan Kaufman/Elsevier.

Chapter 6

Few, Stephen, 2006. *Information Dashboard Design: The Effective Visual Communication of Data*, p. 119. Analytics Press. ISBN 0-596-10016-7.

Shneiderman, Ben, 1992. "Tree Visualization with Tree-Maps: 2-D Space-Filling Approach," *ACM Transactions on Graphics*, 11:92–99. doi:10.1145/102377.115768. hdl:1903/367.

Tufte, Edward, 1990. *Envisioning Information*. Graphics Press, p. 67. ISBN 978-0961392116.

Tufte, Edward, line chart, https://www.edwardtufte.com/bboard/q-and-a-fetch-msg?msg_id=0001OR&topic_id=1&topic=.

Tufte, Edward, 2006. *Beautiful Evidence*. Graphics Press, p. 47. ISBN 0-9613921-7-7.

Wilkinson, Leland and Michael Friendly, May 2009. "The History of the Cluster Heat Map," *The American Statistician*, 63(2): 179–184. *CiteSeerX* 10.1.1.165.7924. doi:10.1198/tas.2009.0033.

Chapter 7

Designing Better Maps: A Guide for GIS Users (2nd ed.). New York, Redland CA: Esri Press, 2016.

Dartmouth Medical School (Author), 1999, April 1. "The Quality of Medical Care in the United States: A Report on the Medicare Program," *The Dartmouth Atlas of Health Care 1999*.

Chapter 8

Kosara, 2016. https://eagereyes.org/blog/2016/an-illustrated-tour-of-the-pie-chart-study-results.

Tractinsky, Noam and Joachim Meyer, 1999. "Chartjunk or Goldgraph? Effects of Presentation Objectives and Content Desirability on Information Presentation," *MIS Quarterly* 23(3): 397–420. Accessed May 16, 2020. doi:10.2307/249469.

Chapter 9

https://www.census.gov/content/dam/Census/library/publications/2018/demo/p70-152.pdf.

Chapter 10

Few, Stephen, 2013. *Information Dashboard Design: The Effective Visual Communication of Data*, p. 26. Analytics Press. ISBN-13: 978-1938377006; ISBN-10: 1938377001.

Chapter 11

Cairo, Alberto, 2013. *The Functional Art: An Introduction to Information Graphics and Visualization*. New Riders Press.

Malamed, Connie. "Infoposters Are Not Infographics: A Comparison," http://understandinggraphics.com/visualizations/infoposters-are-not-infographics/.

Offenhuber, D., 2010. "Visual Anecdote." *Leonardo*, 43(4): 367–374, https://doi.org/10.1162/LEON_a_00010. 10.1162/LEON_a_00010 [Google Scholar].

Closing Thoughts

Duckworth, Angela, 2016. *Grit: The Power of Passion and Perseverance*. New York: Scribner.

Ericsson, K. Anders, 2009. *Development of Professional Expertise: Toward Measurement of Expert Performance and Design of Optimal Learning Environments*. Cambridge University Press. ISBN-13: 978-0521518468; ISBN-10: 0521518466.

Index

Note: Page references followed by 'f' refer to Figures